vert (vərt), n: In English forest law
everything within a forest that grows
and bears a green leaf that may serve
as cover for deer. v: To turn, to turn
over (as in the ground).

Also by Catherine Staples

*The Rattling Window*

*Never a Note Forfeit*

# VERT

*Poems*

Catherine Staples

MERCER UNIVERSITY PRESS
Macon, Georgia

MUP/ P690

Published by Mercer University Press
1501 Mercer University Drive
Macon, Georgia 31207

28 27 26 25 24    5 4 3 2 1

Books published by Mercer University Press are printed on acid-free paper that meets the
requirements of the American National Standard for Information Sciences—Permanence of Paper
for Printed Library Materials.

Printed and bound in the United States.

This book is set in Adobe Caslon Pro.

Cover art: "Metamorphis," Suzanne Stryk.

Cover/jacket design by Burt&Burt.

ISBN    978-0-88146-921-9
Cataloging-in-Publication Data is available from the Library of Congress

*For Paul*


*and for James, Claire,*
*Natalie, and Kevin*

MERCER UNIVERSITY PRESS

*Endowed by*

TOM WATSON BROWN
*and*
THE WATSON-BROWN FOUNDATION, INC.

I long ago lost a hound, a bay horse, and a turtledove, and am still on their trail. Many are the travellers I have spoken concerning them, describing their tracks and what calls they answered to.
—HENRY DAVID THOREAU


White ticking of the cricket in the grass. Companionable answering. Two whispering like that as long as you listen.
—EAMON GRENNAN

# Contents

*With Rocks and Stones and Trees*

# Dear Henry,

Henry Thoreau who has been at his father's since the death of his
brother was ill and threatened with *lockjaw!* his brother's disease.
  –*Ralph Waldo Emerson*

Like Achilles smearing his face with soot,
shearing his hair at the news of Patroclus's death,
you, too, took a step to the world of the dead
when your brother died. Bewildered,
your jaw and limbs stiffened with his.
Then it ended—like floodwaters, it subsided.
You were alive. His memory, a bright
vein of quartz looping through granite,
a glinting diagonal, unsullied and intact
within you. Oblique, flashing—
                              you leapt
the Emersons' back stairs, two at a time,
rat-a-tat of a stick on a railing, children
like capes in your wake, you found the first
huckleberries, tamed the woodchuck. Borrowed
the ax, built the cabin, played your brother's flute.
You drew the oars, then let them go.
Dear invisible, dear true,
with every endeavor, you held him close.
You swallowed the long winter—
and his lost vigor flew through you.

# Vert

As in green, *vert,* a royal demesne
stocked with deer. *Invert* as in tipped
as a snow globe, going nowhere in circles
but not lost, not bereft as the wood
without deer, waiting for the white antlered
buck, or his does, or any slim yearling
to step along the berm, return. *Vertigo*
as in whirling round, *swimming in the head,*
unanchored by the long spring,
the horse cantering, the meadow dropping
like an elevator into the earth, falling
like Persephone through a crevice, a swiveling
crack, a loose screw, a lost way. *Disordered*
as in *death lasts,* my brother's not coming back.
The spin of it continuous as in looking down
from height, and then it stops, the *spinning*
just slows, a chariot wheel stilled in grass.
The world is the same, but it isn't. The tipped
views of trees when hanging from your knees.
The deer in twos and threes watching.

# Diana-of-the-Crosswinds

If she hadn't moved, she'd have spun for you—
there below your window. The first statue

to be lit by lights. If she hadn't moved,
she'd still be there in the chalk-blue cold

over the old Madison Square where Harry
cleared eight feet with Snowman. No, the chronology

is all wrong. You and I weren't yet alive
when the weathervane spun—who knows what time

is like where you are? We'd have loved to see
the Amish horse saved from slaughter, to believe

he'd run from a seller, tire tied to him, leaping
fences, home in time for dinner, shape-shifting

from champion to summer companion when children
swam him in the sound. Is time like that? Can you blend

days and places, is death a weathervane of choices?
Can you pass through ages like garden hedges?

Or are you ice, wind, lichen spinning with earth,
drawn like a tide filling our bay,
                        oh,
                                anything but inert.

# Lake

Midsummer thick with blackberry, bindweed.
     A yellow moon banked in fog
         until swans appeared, far side

         of the lake. We lifted our heads, drew
    breath, our strides easing like thoroughbreds
in the comfort of pines. The lake breathing

in quick slaps, the moon's face breaking in waves—
     then just like that—the swans were gone.
        I turned to answer your look

        but you were the lake—
    mirror of hills and trees, keeper of swans.
Your death undone for a white minute.

Each night in the forest of sleep—
    *finda, finnen, fundevogel,*
        a sort of singing while crying cry.

        Like the forester who found
    a child in the crown of an oak,
I sometimes hear you in daylight—

a red-winged blackbird singing past me
    cattail to cattail swaying, waiting,
        rising like a red thread in thin air,

        a repeating halo of wings.
    Three times the wonder
in summer's heavy air—then the heron

lifting wings too wet too wide
      languorous low—might, never   no
          she holds—the lake a glittering go of ripples.

## In a Hurry

It's the peeling birch and the lake glimpsed through it,
sheets buckling in wind, the emerald seams of moss
between pavers, three children rounding a bend.
Sky bluer than vetch, a small hare on the garden path
deciding and the lake roiled, her waves no longer
steadily east but blown hard to the far side. Beyond
evergreens edged with gorse before the path ends,
the blackberries are humming with dragonflies,
beyond that, the sheep and the hawthorn hedge
where the rain has not yet begun, where the thrush
move in and out of wind in the quiet that is theirs,
where music begins and body skates with mind's
sweet whim. It's beauty oblique as wooden shutters
close on a seam of light and a husband's glance travels
like a fox on a path staring back, will you follow?

# Sheep and Angels

It's early yet, the sun's low.
The three-rail fence casts a crazy
shadow, rangy phantasmagoria,
crooked and impossibly long.

Hundreds of days fly by, one thing
keeps. Rounding the corner by
the old schoolhouse, it's that craggy
sheep—four-square, sturdy, alert.

What is it he sensed? Last
of the night coyotes, peeling off
in pairs, the here-now-gone
damp edging a new cut of hay?

Daylight is skeptical as the rest
of the flock. You tap your chest
with the gesture of our grandfather,
just this, here and here, that worries you.

A phantom prick of something
where the dark mass gathered
before the chemicals blasted
you free and clear.

But here you are before me, handsomely
present: delicate light lines of hair,
eyebrow, and beard growing in, here
in the Italian place with the good bread

and oil, we're talking about our children.
The winter sunlight munificent

as the turn, Broadway to Madison,
the clean, clear lines of the park trees.

On the way home I see these long-faced
beauties rising from the pedestal
on Farragut's statue, from a sea
of stone they rise—what solemn

promises—things they know, things
they won't say. Guardians, I'd like
to think, bluestone angels
who might be sworn to keep you safe.

# Like the First Horses, Pegan Hill

A late gallop home through the fields, blue Vespa
on a run of cobbled stone through Red Hook.
Square shoulders with hips, frictional grip,
heels down we find our lines. Never closer

on a run of cobbled stone by Valentino pier.
*Don't lean,* you shout into the rumbling air.
Heels down we find our lines, never closer,
shoulder to shoulder, we arrow loose and fly.

*Don't lean,* we breathe the deep rumbling sea.
Flare of damp, the salt waves peak and recede.
Shoulder to shoulder, herring gulls twist and fly.
Whip of light through the trees, sun in our eyes.

Kettle of heat. The gardens peak, recede—
this fig, that plum, the Madonnas in alcoves.
Whip of light in the leaves, hair in our eyes.
We lean hard into August, last of the blue

plums and figs, those shy does in coves of pine.
Square shoulders with hips, frictional grip.
We lean hard into the first horses, last light.
A late gallop home through the blue hay, your Vespa.

# Anthropocene

Like a promise made, forgotten,
remembered, or a portent out of season—

these starlings rise like a single thought.
A hundred or more lift from shorn corn,

settle like a siege in the lone beech.
The sun gives signs, so, too, the birds.

The wood thrush diminished, the bell
of her doubled syrinx thinning each spring.

Honeybees are disappearing, leaving
their queens. Is it Virgil's script or Yeats'

as the dispossessed stream from cities,
children on their hips, and starlings

tip, gyre, and volute away, each striking
their own sharp glint like winter sun

catching on the blade of a ceremonial axe:
a bright wide flickering, a sound as low

as bees' wings fanning the comb, groundswell
of thunder before it begins, murmuration

they call it—the sweep of many moving as one.

# The Arrow of the Angel Had Gone Too Deep

*–Ralph Waldo Emerson*

The deep wound of not having a brother,
perpetual ache in the shoulder's blade,
the bare plateau where scapula
might attach to coverts if ever once
we had wings. There at the rib's ledge:
the severing place, a hollow, a gouge
and, ever after, a smoothed-over scar.
Just so, lichen scars a rock, blankets
the hollow places where rain collects,
ribs them in wings and florets, gray-green
coverts where algae and fungus thrive
a bare plateau, immune to heat and drought
and sorrow, the perpetual ache in the shoulder's
blade, the deep wound of losing your brother.

## What Lasts

      Above all,
the red-winged blackbird.
His whistled trill
and the long after—

there's distance in it,
heat and light,
all the places we've loved.
The deer are skittish

grace, faltering
prayers leaping away.
Not so the blackbird—
never a note forfeit

as we come close.
He holds the line steady
through arc and dive,
*Oka-leee*—and echo

over the inland sea.
Fescue, foxtail, flax,
wave on wave, violet,
hay-blue, then a sudden

whirling swathe of white.
Something in this meadow
takes us back summers
to windy Lamma Island,

curling path to a hip bone
of white sand: nest home
of the Hong Kong green
sea turtles. Remember

the volcanic rock
shaping the bay? A glacier's
work, the drowned sea risen;
earth's sweet continuance—

all these cousins
leaping from the prow.
And now blackbirds
prolific—look here

a saucer of marsh grass
hidden by cattails,
a second clutch of blue
scrawled with brown script.

# All This Water and Wind

The sound of wind exhaling through the trees
  and upper heavens, the long blow—something

    begun in another hemisphere?
And catching now in the crowns of oaks, belling

  buoys along the coast—headland and cove
    mapped by crosswinds. The iron ring

of the bell's tongue, not a language we know.
  And here, inland, the inconstant wind chime

  in the crabapple barely registers.
The cochlea knocking so lightly it's

  no more than the exodus of ants from
    house to woods. But our bodies are water.

In northern bays, channel markers lean in
  carrying the news. Each coast bears currents

    and any sailor knows that the minder
at the tip of the mast—fitful, wild

  tells nothing of the deep, it speaks only of wind.
    Whales hove and dive and roll like horses

in pastures, buckling and turning. Beautiful
  hulks collapsing, changing, they right themselves

    and go under ice floes blue as the cold
that held them. Ice sheets shrink. Glaciers ride

the sea in floods of freshwater, channel
　　markers pitch, ringing in the steep.

But we hear weather, not words, not warning. Gulls drift
　　volition-less—then arrow away. Sunlit and

　　blue, on a day like this one the planes flew.

# When Orpheus Sang

The wild things gathered: lynx and lion,
red fox and otter. Oak and linden moved—
imagine it's true. What if myth hid science
too subtle to be discerned, alder, willow
whitening as before a storm, listening in,
listing. Sorrow sung well becomes beauty—
full of yearning, hurt, and desire. Think of
the fox in the corn, lost to hound voices
hearkening, anguished, all the long hollow.
Their cries close in and still he waits—
that dire proximity, call it psalm
song, the dying fall of spheres, sounding
below on slopes, leaves, scree—
who wouldn't rest hands and chin
on a still rake or pause in the dusty road?
Who's to know if such singing might move
a grove of trees, might carry a loss even
halfway home? What if the lyric isn't ours
alone, but primordial as the maker's ladder,
winding through blood and bone, the murmuring green.

*Fury*

# Book of Hours

The hummingbird in its smallness:
      little whirr in my ear as my brother
and I walk Burrough—
      I keep hearing it.
          This place is a broad swathe of light,
crease and fold of seven mountains going away.

Wind blows things far apart,
      even the deer appear singly.
There's no intimate tug, a sudden memory
         flushing up
      the way of warm thermals
         closing round;
      it's a church bell calling and gone.

The resurrected don't gather here—
   lily pods profuse in the flat glass
         of the dark pond,
      watery roots tangled pleasantly,
inextricably with their neighbors.
      The living-on souls travel high—
         not shoulder to shoulder
but solo in cold drafts
         rising with a single hawk,
burnished gold, lonely.

My brother sees it differently.
      This is Burrough—
         steep hillside and meadow,
stands of birch and wild runs of blueberry.
      He brings the children up for campfires,
         long nights zippered in

under shallow green tents,
contours of the surrounding hills
grown sharp with coyotes
calling peak to peak.

He's wondering if the pump
still works; we crank the handle
and walk the lines, marveling
how each stone has kept its fit,
roughed up by lichen,
seamed by moss.

Sheep pasture we're guessing—
the low crown of trees, flourish
of bayberry, wild rose, juniper.
I tell him the hillside would tame
with one or two ponies;
he's quiet—not that he doesn't remember
our ease with the horses.
It's good to be beside him,
a companionable silence,
the off the on, the hushed whirr of wings.

# Wearing His Shoes

As someone you love lies dying—
you want breath, heart, head, and eyes
to thread and thrum steady with yours, uncanny
splice, a good enough fit. And this is why
you slip into his shoes. Your arch the ache
for flesh—for a sibling you can't yet let go.
The feel of his heels scudding along hall floors:
noisy announcement of not gone. Your lungs,
his heart. Not since twenty have you run like this—
ice, wind, breath. Each sweet lengthening, hip,
thigh, calf, the drum of running,
the beautiful illusion of two as one, leaping
the stairs, two at a time, love you, love you more—
rounding the corner, opening the door.

# In the Windy Room

Curtains buckle and fly. The sky is
    marbled, ragged scraps of debris

tumble for the sea. God has gone off
    somewhere—it's too hard this—

the current of your breath
    ebbs, everyone's in bed with you.

Beyond the glass—a host
    of warblers in swaying trees, a rest

before departure: sotto voce, novices
    at the Dominican priory. The call

of voices singing aisle to aisle.
    They asked us to carry the gifts

that Christmas. Here in the windy room
    a minister is speaking about light—

choosing light, no talk of Christ.
    Already the cold waves bloom

and fall—there—where sea longs
    to blur with sky, a sharp and beautiful blue.

You're still here, steadfast, trying—
    borne like a leaf on the flood of our song.

# The Oldest Dream

We are in the small cabin, more
tree fort than house, the light
goes everywhere, the open door,
the wooden floor. I am sweeping up

something—sand from the creek?
Beautiful white grit that must have
come up with salamanders beneath
rocks. All morning in the shallows,

barefoot, seeking what we'd
only half seen, the cold thrill of
flipping rocks for a quick Houdini.
Our dire need to see it again—

lithe escape, the sudden empty
imprint of rock, muck rising,
nearly blinding those free
bright stripes of verdigris.

Alive and hidden, pearls of sand,
clear sand in river of wood,
salamander in the palm of a hand.
A tree fort in a windstorm

riding it out, intact. A train
whistle from far away, the small
tables and chairs, slanting light,
your small hands, the plain

song of sweeping.

# Fever

I ran in then but won't go now. The room,
the light, the day, your belly distended
with the body's end. The wind and ruin
that will not quit; the fever that meant to rend
illness in two. The body runs on expecting
to win, it fails to understand its ending.
We drew the windows wide, letting
November in, hoping to cool, to mend,
to slake, abate. Even now the mind refuses,
leaves that room for this one: house-in-between
the harbor and the bay. How slowly the mind loses
loss, your children asleep in its rooms, its makeshift
summer beds where rigging snaps masts and last scenes
list and fall as catboats rock on their moorings.

# Landmarks, Compass

The long winter took all the boxwoods,
    plenty of wrens.

But not the warblers: redstarts, magnolias
    riding the cold fronts south.

Hatch-year blackpolls yield to the pull
    of the poles, ear for surf,

eye on the coast, the shape it makes
    under the clouds.

In the blowing cold, things simplify:
    cliffside, spinney, creek.

The upper meadow topping with phlox,
    corridors through milkweed.

A lone stone pine gusting in sea wind.

    *

First time I saw the plaque on Montague,
    we straddled our bikes,

something about Auden, a transatlantic
    journey in wartime.

It's the sort of thing you look for in dreams—
    the way back, a ruby

crowned kinglet hovering mid-air,

you in the sea-green

light as the ferry blasts and engines
        reverse, there, still there:

broad shouldered, squinting into the bright.

# Hurricane

The harbor hardly sleeps at night, what with
listening in, glittering. Masts hover and sway
while keels answer in watery knocks, their own way
of saying things. Within the house some rift
prevails; my mother opens all the doors but one
to uncover the latest grievance. Fury without
the slamming. By day she smolders with night
truths, eyes downcast under her hat. She won't
speak, can't understand. Her grief needs an enemy.
Orion's belt so low in the summer sky it's ready
to sink like Hector's great spear, bereft of his strength.
We all lost him; it's the unsaid word in each breath.
None of us fit for the wind's work, we'll trust
to the house that took a hurricane, held hard to the isthmus.

# Dear Augustine,

You heard the children's voices
and knew, *tolle lege, tolle, lege.*
Was it syllable & sound that wooed you?

The ancient pull of music over matter like *Red Rover,*
*Red Rover, send Augie right over.* Shirts billowing,
the good rush of wind. Like love of Latin,

hatred of Greek, a child's clarity cuts through
the din deciding. God's voice tumbling like eggs
a-rattle in boiling water, sweet tumult

of the first kitchen, fogging the windows,
dimming the high pane over the door.
You were waiting in that place past grief.

Perhaps it was nothing you heard—
just your sorting mind, sorting
one of childhood's refrains.

Like hearing your name in cold air
a reddening flush climbing the limbs.
They're daring you to break the line,

to pass through the kingdom of grasped hands,
far side, offside, out of kilter echoing.
Nothing ever the same after this—

by what miracle do they know your name?

# Souls Rising: A Crown

*For my brother and the horse*

## Feeding the Hounds

On Cato Lane, a pot of bluefish ghosts a low
boil. Simmer and mist, a pre-thunder rumbling,
the bones come clean as whitened souls.
By hand, she lifts the filigree of spine, ravels
loose the symmetry of flesh from rib, works
warm fish into dry kibble. The kitchen's wreathed
in fog; it smells oddly like supper. Hounds clamor
and leap as she walks out to feed them. A phone
rings on in the empty kitchen. Miles off, another farm,
the vet will draw the dose, our good brown horse
will go down slowly, knees and hocks folding,
white petals of apple scattering, chickens thrumming
in his ears, the low hum of sleep approaching,
the wide sky going somewhere unexpected.

## Low Hum of Sleep

The wide sky takes you in, breath goes
loose of ribs. Currents of wind whip
until wind is all there is. And clouds, cold
veils brushing by. A sudden yearning
to be the red-tail gliding in his spheres, unharried
by the crows below in crowns of pine.
Here, there is only to think a thing, it happens.
Comfort of thermals, wings spread wide,
primary from primary, fanned, and paper-thin.
Serpentines in the upper meadow become
inventions in air, one loop spurs another: shim,
glint, and vanish. The ones you once loved
looking up, admiring, but not really seeing;
already you're fit for quickness, a new Eden.

# Where the Harrier Flew

An Eden in air, a thundering quickness—
imagine a clothesline of shirts along the bay
taken up in gusts, billowing wild. Take away
the shirts, see the souls clear as jellyfish
in the Atlantic? Thin crimson ribbing, light
passing through. Rising, always rising,
new souls like phosphor climbing the heights.
Luminous, my brother layers his dress shirts,
clothes his airy thinness in blues, pinks, stripes.
We're singing coyotes down from their ranges,
making angels fly, there, in the sap-house, flare
of souls burning bright as tinder. Maple distills
like rain on a lake, a sweetness layers the air.


# A Horse at the Half-Door

A sweetness layers the air, night's chorus
thins to wind. You are gone and the horse
stands at the door. His head lifts—a bluster
of nickering—then slowly lowers to my palm.
One hand on his withers, I make the vault
upward, bareback, first try; together we watch
the clouds fly. He's quiet but not calm.
He understands what he can, I bow my chin
to his shoulder, breathing in the noiseless
cloister of mud and sweat and hay. The horse
knows something of sorrow, its wilderness
of waiting. He listens for the scraping haul
of a swinging door, the timbre of your voice.

## Like a Grove of Trees

The timbre of your voice sounds when it can't.
Does the mind insist or are you here in sunlight,
candlelight, wind? On a porch in Bishop, Georgia
your gravelly tenor is the iron ring of the forge,
wood burn and flame. Is it your will or ours
believing you're here now, listening to wedding vows,
blessing the hour? Your glasses glint and cast
about the room like a chandelier's light, you last
through seasons like a grove of trees, the creased
bright Pleiades. Stand in for the missing priest.
Summon the Madonna, one slender foot in
our world, the other resplendent in heaven.
Let night and light wrap them in folds, the blue
bridal clothes—her dreamy idylls, her harsh truths.

# Bloodroot

When a house is gone from the land,
the walls fallen, foundation a sleeping ruin,
earth turns to her work, mortar thins to marl and sand.

Fieldstones balance in a rough-stacked stand
until they can't, tumbling past nettle, henbit.
When a house succumbs to lines of land—

who will miss the breadth a chimney spanned
where sheep now graze and spiders spin?
Earth quickens, a spring sifts through rock and sand.

Hawks loop where smoke rose in a thick band,
hung along the heavens, left with the wind.
When a house is gone from the land—

a groundhog rises on his hind feet, an offhand
pivot, he looks and looks. Sun, wind, and rain.
Earth turns to erasing, creating. The wrens dive in.

Cattails, flurry of wings, a splintered band
of red-winged blackbirds returns to wetland.
When a house is gone, earth turns to her work:
Bloodroot. Singing. The world spins on like sand.

*Survivors*

# Marathon

Remember that part where Gilgamesh
tries to outrun the sun and does so—hour
by double hour—he flouts the natural order.

What would it be to race past winter
into the June of arrowwood viburnum?
Might all be well by then? Beaded in

berries so beloved by waxwings, fragrant
as allspice deep in the wood. Look now
the shriveled brown petals gone to ground.

The chrysalis you can't see. The world is
burying itself in leavings, in leaves—
in seeds. It's still churning sunlight to gold

albeit slowly. Imagine the oblique sidewise
vision of Gilgamesh if he raced not a day
but a season. Past fallen stem, pale stalks,

imagine the shimmering cloak of color. Stride
by stride, umber and dun turning viridian,
a gas-lit spectrum of greens. Imagine

chlorophyll with a body as fluent as any
coywolf in the clearing, fast thinking, sly—
hue of dunes and lit sand, then dark as pines.

Luminous as the tipped heel of Orion,
an animal aliveness, an urgent will to survive.
I am listening for wind through the closed

windows. I have left off reading—
you are light on the shoulders of Gilgamesh
fleeing the earthly city. I am watching

it happen, the fleet bloom of greening,
the time lapse of calves and thighs,
hour by double hour, outracing the sun.

# Wreck of the Jason

The iron schooner broke clean in two... and the waves
rushed over her stern which sank like lead into the sand.
*Truro, 1893*

It's little he knew or thought
he knew, there in the sand
stumbling, hardly upright,
the sea still in him, her wrack
and swell. On all fours,
recollecting the din in
the rigging: the audible
crack as the keel split.
Heart astonished
by permeable borders.
The others gone under.
They hadn't his luck,
was it the bale of jute
or the sleek bob of a seal's
head that righted his way?
Surely some supernal
rhythm fixed his course.
He washed up on shingle,
frozen, bleary with sleet.
White as clouds, the souls flew.

For weeks he heard it—the terrible
slatting of sails on spars.
Nothing stopped it—only
the rhythm of hooves,
the Truro milk horse, tin-shake
of harness as he stepped out
in the cold yard and the mare

dropped her craggy head.
He smoothed the length
of her ears, forefinger
to thumb, loosened the scruff,
and there at his chest,
a warm blow of breath.

# Moonblind

Overnight the white pony is wizened, good eye sewn shut
after a kick or a nail. The other eye is moonblind:

better, then worse as the crescent thins. On a good day
it once tracked the flit of movement; now it's a still pool,

unwitting mirror of a world he can't see. Last night snow,
now gusting mist. Today's a washout loss to be blind.

Snow so bright the shadows seem sculpted, the dark godly,
illumined as when Jonah is tossed and field on field

of sea flattens: glitter of moon in shallow troughs.
Surely, he knew before it happened, fleet register in

the treble of spine, in birches edging the meadow.
A slump thunders from a failing roof. Sidelined, blind,

still, he lifts his whiskered chin to the blow of white.
A microcosm shivers through whale-dark days. Snow scrims

the valley of his sunken eye, glitter pricks each lash in ice,
translated, shriven. For all we know, seer of our

falling forests, a mind like winter quickening in wind.

# Henry Beston at the Outermost House

After the rut of war, you sunk your faith in fairy tales,
writing one after another, but the solace
was makeshift—so with good New England wood,

you built a house in sand on Nauset Spit.
A place to come, come summer, two rooms,
ten windows. A well pipe to water

under the dunes, chimney to warm the rooms,
oil lamps, candles, and a maw of driftwood.
A simple lookout on sea and marsh.

With every intention of staying a fortnight
you lasted a year. The roar of the sea
held you, rhythm of the great waves

breaking in threes. Daily the ebb tide
delivered its due: sea grass and rockweed,
bleached skulls of seals, then half an oar,

a horseshoe crab gutted with sand.
Barehanded you lifted him by the spire
of his tail, rinsing him in waves,

until the hundred whip-like cilia
were motion again. Each night the beam
of Nauset light swept across your wall.

*

On the morning my grandfather walks the beach,
you balance mid-rung on the coast guard's
borrowed ladder, hammering down shingles,

readying for winter. You've thrown your lot in
with the solitary hawk who harries you
down the beach. *Circus hudsonius*

skimming the blue-black, infinitely slow rollers.
Probably a nest, far side of the marsh.
On that day, she nearly sends you

toppling from the roof with the close call
of battering wings. Over beers in the lantern
you'll recall the assault of her attentions

as hardly amorous, quip about Leda
and the Swan, under stars with the guardsman
on night watch. But just now, you're waist flush

to the roof, double hammering, bare chested, lean;
behind you marsh and mud flat, that rank animal reek,
a phalanx of green fiddlers gone sideways into the reeds.

# The January Pear

Yes, but you sent the Asian pear when least
I expected—

subtle fattening on the shorn antlers of the bare
espalier. Winter light an odd nurse for a thriving bole.

Some trick of shadow hid it, that or the long grey days
without a horse. Somehow I missed its beginning.

Birchbark, kindling stared back in flame and woodsmoke
singed my hair. All the while under sun and moon

the pear grew through March, size of a plum stone. Deer
passed by, even the squirrels, those thieves, let it be—

each morning its presence belled the quiet and I knew
you were there, thin as a handkerchief in a hip pocket,

whistlely as a wren with instruction. No, it wasn't
just your voice in my ear, its distinct nasal cadence,

but the tangible pear. And even now that it's gone on,
and the tree on which it grew is burning with bloom,

I have only to look out the window to see you.
In the habit of looking, the shape lives: the orb

from which the wren flew, now a white fist
of six blooms, each anther tipped rose, rose-white

before darkening to seed, love redeemed
where the pear appeared, ochre and green.

# Wings Neck to Nobska

First bacon, then crackers.
All for the salt. A string
of beach towels and wet clothes
stretched cross the line.
Soon enough the wind
will answer. Surely
the dog's head will do
for a seal's—
when her ears lay flat
and the angle's right.
Cicadas rise stepwise,
a sweet racket
that hums and rises

then goes. Just slips
into the murmur,
fluent with bees
in the chives.
Wind snaps a flagpole,
and it's mainsheet on mast
ringing. A bay of sails.
Deep within, a stir
loosens, ice knocks
channels, fans rattle.

First time the call is faint
as a watermark.
Shipwreck, ten, eleven,
still my husband
and the children sleep.
Twice, as the dog sighs
under the pears.

Third time; it's dead clear.
The foghorn sounding
over the water,
whitening widening
into their limbs,
lip, hair, breath—
it's bringing in the deep,
a heartbeat at a time.

*Fog, mist, rock*: the foghorn
calls over the channel.

Another answers:
*ebb tide at quarter.*
The channel markers
are leaning in, listening.
*You mustn't know,*
*no, let the house sleep—*
*and children dream*
*while the buoys bell*
*their whitecapped, rushed ways.*

Near and far, two horns
din breadth and width.
But we're no sailors
and their simple songs
draw us on under
keels, over wrecks.
Shimmer of an anchor's fluke,
lost moorings, the thin blue
shreds of a spinnaker.
A deep and frightening
beauty over earth
under sea.
The clarity of ridged sand,

slow rock of anemone,
plain truths.
Magnificent, how the cold
goes through you.

# The Heavy Lift of Wings

No myth, there you were
In the lone oak, fledged, new.
Poised and immaculate.
Nothing like an angel, sinew

And beak, the curved scimitar
Of intention. You waited
Past reason. A hawk's eye
Took me in, sunlight flashed

And dimmed, bluebirds swept
Tree to tree—your name,
I called your name as you lifted
Away and I knew you in your change.

# Four Days at Ten Below

Like a sleeve of Arctic air—
the way you meet the chill in a cold
house on leaving the warmth of husband,
tangled limbs, and quilt. Step forward:
there before you an unattached shadow
glacial and patient, a half-step ahead
of heat you've carried from the bed.
Rush to the hearth to light a fire
with kindling and birchbark, fumbling
in the icy stupor of a house without heat.
Four days at ten below—the cold
comes closer. The dog begins to bleat
in her sleep. Maybe death is like this,
a hairsbreadth away, always in the offing,
but for a guardian at your back. Vigilant,
wings thrumming like an owl's, sheathed
in feathers, a batten closing on the weft.
Her rhythmic silk repels the cold as
the first flame wavers blue, leaps white,
a slow translucent flickering. The dog
lifts her eyes, kindling falls to log,
the blaze catches—and the shadow is gone.

# Mycorrhizae

What kind of life is the pine leading now,
      not Lear on the heath or Richard in the tower—
          Is it my father's life at the end of life?

The slowed down heartbeat of a northern bear,
      slumbers broken by sharp waking, eyes
          wide with the self that resides within?

When lightning struck our white pine, a fissure
      halved her, rain of needles in our neighbor's
          pool—her verdant green gone rust-red.

Without a crown, her rough beauty undone,
      the tree men scaled her to a high stump.
          Confined, she's nothing like herself.

Her long roots radiate across the yard.
      She roams like a mad starfish under the earth,
          some roots surface, hard as sea ropes with salt.

They tip above the lawn, nearly trip me
      as I head out with peels of beet to feed
          the compost. Teabags, carrots—

winter's kindling for the next season's feast:
      a butternut fattening unseen, a wasp
          buried in the heart of a fig.

All morning, the fire. I watch it blaze a torrent
      of words, a snow-white semblance.
          Singe of lichen spackles a fallen branch.

The fire keeps. My father sleeps upright
in his chair, I wake him with the old stories.
The scuffed blue rowboat, the beetle cat.

Four of us scrapping for holds on the tiller,
my brother alive, the hair in his eyes.
The wind picks up, the centerboard hums.

Hard-a-lee, hairsbreadth to the wintry channel,
all we'd never know flying beneath us.

# Wild Apples

It was the close hold of the Emerson stairwell
brought them to mind, wild apples shot up
from rocky hillsides and brimming with fruit.
A fleet thunder of heels, bright corridor
of coming and going. Run of railings like
saplings, green, gold crescents on wallpapered
walls shimmering like lanterns, like a river
at night alive with stars. Long-legged, fit,
he walked the tip of a fallen pine, held the boat
steady as each of us stepped into the sway.
Fireflies unsheeted the dark, the quick lines
of willows, the inlet where mallards fledged.
Honeysuckle and whippoorwill, there in the stairwell.
The scuffed green bow and the two masts passing
Bittern Cliff to Fairhaven. Flat sheen of stars
on still water, then the sudden seeing in—
as if slipping like a pickerel amid the lightnings
of fireflies, flitting past Orion's bow, his bent knee.
The northern star backlit through river grass.

# After Seeing the Irish Modern Dance Theatre's Lear

First light is breaking
beyond the donkey's pasture.
Inside the darkened house
brightness rims the shutters.

Sunlight strains before it breaks,
fattens to a saffron seam.
A saint's pageant flashes
and slides across the room.

Morning runs riot—
a tumbler's leap of shadows.
A chandelier rides the ceiling,
the writing desk blanches

in the changed light—shivers
and stares. All of it quick
as lakewater dried in your hair,
a flame blown loose from the wick.

# Dear Hesiod,

Some say three, others nine. Varro claimed
      one was born of water, another played daylight

like wind, invisible as the airs on Caliban's isle.
      A third made a home of the human voice singing.

Dear Hesiod, perhaps it wasn't the Muses
      you glimpsed on sodden farm fields,

barefoot, sopping wet—
      just a few village girls and cousins.

Lashes of rain, blowing mist, their arms
      linked wrist by wrist

until they broke and sang. And a great haul
      of wind shook the crowns of trees,

leaves twisting white, a bough cracked high.
      You heard it—a shadow swayed and fell.

A red fox fairly flew through, his umber tail
      flaming like the Perseids. Was it then

you knew you were never alone—
      the voice welling up wasn't strictly *yours*?

The girls gone. There under the dripping trees
      a herd of deer, eight or nine at least.

# Godspeed

Not fly away, but steady along, the good
stretch: hip flexor and quad, the tensile length
of the long reach loosely swinging forward.
Heel to heel on Hicks, on Remsen, the strength
of your legs aligns with mine—impossible.
You're gone and away as a humpback's fluke
sounding the Hudson. Still, some sibling-thin proof
fires like a synapse—and I know you in the lull
unseeable, electric,
                   you lean and fly—I bend
slipping through the promenade crowds, transfixed
by dinosaur diggers, tugs chugging. Suspended
above the diesel tumult of unearthing, green, and sea,
I pause with the sparrows on the railing, take respite
in this, your last wilderness, its vast and shifting frieze.

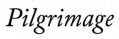

*Pilgrimage*

# If the Room Spoke Back

*The Old Manse, Concord, MA*

Would anyone hear it—
the hearth mouthing the language
    of flames in summer, small


    rips of wind in still air? Would anyone
passing through these rooms—
    wheel on their heels, return


    to the slim something in air,
not knowing that wallpaper,
    desk chair, and andirons all conspired


    to tell the house's book of hours,
her glossy minutes, the infant's
    long fingers, the cousin's penciled


    sketches on the bedroom wall?
Some days simple as grains of rice,
    others wider than the children's


    palms spanned on the wavy glass
as they watched things happen.
    Even the damselfly alighted

on the sill's edge is rapt,
wings closed, her iridescent blue
        darkening like a storm


        as if she too knew the history,
the militia on the bridge,
        the children at the windows,


        the smoke and thunder of guns.
The children's father in the field
        deciding. Their mother's voice


        in waves, over the turned
earth, calling him in.
        The minutemen


        who didn't especially intend
for all of this to begin,
        the children at the glass waiting.

# Palimpsest

Sophia's script on the window's pane, then his,
her diamond's point as pen. Nine months

married in this place—surely they knelt
on the couch, hip by hip in the Old Manse.

*This is my husband's study, 1843,* Sophia wrote
as if to christen Nathaniel's work, their life,

she in her upstairs room painting, and he
below at the hand-hewn desk *in the gold light,*

writing themselves onto landscape,
transcribing apples, pears, apples

far as the eye can see. His hand on the nape
of her neck, their words writ on glass,

on grass, on cloud. Now their sky is ours
so that any of us walking through these rooms

and looking out might see it, one fair hour
new in marriage, the orchard as witness.

# Oster, Oxter

That the hollow above the collarbone
should share its origin with the armpit

seems a linguistic confusion. The one
a way station where kisses might pool

like rainwater, *óster, óst,* along the clavicle
ridge; the other ripe with morning's labor,

two heels on the lug, rocking the shovel
deep, deeper, rhythmically turning earth.

Sharp beads of sweat, proof of intent.
First the daylilies, then the rose. Dozens

of seeds where rows of dying, spent
boxwoods stood. Jimmied loose, lugged away,

cracking at it each day, the body's wheeling
confidence with the right sort of work:

the good labor of tilling and planting earth,
auguries of night, kisses along the clavicle's rim.

# In the Yellow House Attic

Lift the latch with its tin rattle, climb the stairs.
Milkweed, swamp pink. Any chance chickadee
sweeping in through the open window might take
her time deciding—a half-dozen mosses lining the sill.
See the watermarks? Henry loves to watch them green
after dying back. Sheep sorrel, lupine, chickweed.
Yesterday's harvest ferried home in his hat—
the reason the attic smells like a meadow.
That curio more sleeping snake than shell?
Ammonite. Earth, says Henry, is *no lifeless fossil*
*pressed strata on strata*. No museum, no relic—
but a lightly breathing room the birds fly through.
A living core, a humming joist of honey and bees.
A fat clump of moss in the beak of a chickadee.

# Graffiti

We wrote our names in order—
on broom closet walls, fogged in windows.
Sophia and Nathaniel etched theirs
in glass, Emerson's looping script
incised in a desk drawer and young Eddy
Simmons drew freehand on attic walls.
The Manse was his, too, christened in
images: catfish, rat, honeybee—wings
outspread, top of the stairs where
Sophia Peabody brought Nathaniel Hawthorne
and they chose the smaller bedroom.
Serpentines and eights in summer fields
where Nipmuc camped and fished,
arrowheads persist in fields of rye.
*Grass-ground-river* where strokes
curved then disappeared like otters.
An incised line on wet clay. Eel pots
and creels. Clam feasts, a hidden
sunken midden, a ribbed bar of sand
in the river's changing course.
                    Knock of oars
in wooden rests, rap of the bank
on Henry's Musketaquid, the carry
of his flute in the starless dark.
Then the child in utero, Una, loose
of her waters, born in the wedding bed.
The infant nursed, Sophia's bedclothes
shifted like waves—the outdoors entered in.
Time stilled, raveled loose, looped back.
The time of children, the time before.
Nathanial labored at the hand-hewn desk
Henry had fashioned, a perfect height

folding flush to the wall. Behind it,
the bridal bed, wind-dried linen.
Were there too many or not enough
days at the desk? On the riverbanks?
The chill stratum of cold as they all rose
from the water—the held unprintable air.

## Slavery in Massachusetts

Forked shadows of grass on the dry path.
The meadow hardly breathes.
I heard the wasps before I saw them,
high in the trees. If my brother—if John
were here—he'd say not write, the right words.
Plainspoken, broad shouldered, clear—
would he were here to speak against judge,
Governor, and Webster, that devil
of the law's maker. An innocent man,
a fugitive law that sends the free man,
Thomas Sims back to Georgia. Bluets,
celandine, violets: what use is beauty?
I thread my way through rustling oak and
alder, there on the warm hillside of the cut:
*stigmas of hazel*, a dozen crimson rays
breaking from buds like stifled cries
from the hollow. I am halfway to the ponds
on foot—though I will not arrive
in mind. The open air and skit of wind
on water, the free bright light.
They'll take him from jail to dock—
dark purple anthers of elm strew the way.

*Journal, April 1851*

# Every Living Thing

We stood in the room where they slept,
windows facing the race to the sea. Thoreau
would've taken the dimensions at a glance.
But the gruff sound of the interior shutter

hauled across the window's frame,
heave of wood on painted wood, shudder
and cease. What happened to sound
after that? What was wind and what

was sea? The heavy boom and rut
of surf calling all day from the hollow.
Where was it they'd walked that morning?
The look of the heath, wind-blown, combed.

The rising pitch on the way to the sea
shifting by night in their dreams.
The wind raking tracks like a lion's paw,
churning loose a divot of sand, a devil's

whirligig spinning on the spine of Newcomb's
bluff. Ships intimate with the dark—
riding crest to trough. Somewhere a sailor
staring at a compass, another in the rigging

tracking the sweep of Highland's beam
while inside the small room, Thoreau
and Channing slept with wind and waves—
those wreckers of lives—rattling windows,

making bones of ships, timbers from whales.

*Newcombe Cottage, Wellfleet*

# Una Hawthorne on the Picnic Rock

The osprey nests on Fairhaven Bay:
a bedlam of sticks and leaves
threaded through with light and air.
Two or three chicks rise and peer:
swathes of green wave and shake.
Their eyes, thin slits then narrow
keyholes apprising the wide light
and height. Slowly cognizant of shape,
a hundred ways of seeing green.

They wake and sleep and wake
sweetly bewildered, slowly waking
like the young girl who presses herself
flat as she can to the picnic rock
by the river. Lichen scratches but
moss is smooth as thumbs. Her chin
fits here, legs fold into the cleft.

She thinks she can hear the meadow.
No one has yet told her she cannot
hear the meadow, words hatched
in grasses. *Mirror, mirror how
have you been here? Long as
the bear, the cradle. Pennacook,
Nipmuc before deceit and dire
diseases—arrowhead, weaver.*

She thinks the current might carry
her image like a wobbly mirror
far or farther than Egg Rock or
the place where the river widens
to a lake and the osprey are sunk

like stones in their first sleep,
growing flight feathers, storm grey,
ash-white, then a blood-tipped umber.

So many words she doesn't yet know:
*restless, reckless, renegade* so many
syllables from the trees: *naiad, dryad,
naïve,* each word a leaf she sets
on the water, hoping no one will know
she's left the picnic rock. Knee-deep
in sedge, she's chasing a blue darner
through the mucky reeds. The rabbits
nod among themselves. A bee lands
on a keel of penstemon, a violet
chamber opens and on they go.

## Sophia at the Window

The river was in it and the Concord rain.
The child born, the child before, conceived

and lost: *Man's accidents are God's purposes*,
the lines she inscribed on glass,

knowing the womb favors a dress rehearsal,
that words on windows might look through

to the unseeable, like the seventy-year-old
parson who laid out the orchard—dug

the holes, settled the saplings in rows,
spread each loosened ball of roots, tamped

and watered—knew he'd never see fruit,
yet he prepared the room with a view

for the young wife who slipped a diamond
from her narrow finger to still an hour.

She with the hands of a painter, lover,
letter writer, mother. Sophia Hawthorne

back to the fire as Nathaniel read to her.
Apple, peach, pear—a simple, low content.

Child on her hip, sucking her fist, pointing,
as if she too knew Eden when she saw it—

an unmown orchard, a river, the picnic rock;
the glass fogged by wet logs, the glass clear.

# Siblings Beyond the Concord and Merrimack

Partial wing of a horse's track on the path,
disappearing in sand, reappearing in damp
where the wood thrush sang—crystal, lonely—
the bayberry in gaps between trees. Remember
that hound stepped from the wood, one
quick shiver, he shook the shining flecks
from his sides, turned toward us, deliberate,
alert, bright as an island of moss.
Who had he lost that he fell in with us, John?
Stride for stride lifting his head under our palms.

*

It was winter, eight years after you'd gone,
clear as the register of cowbells on hillsides.
An echo of copper—too rhythmic for
a late cow returning, each rung bell, quick
then slow as she stopped to graze, as she
made her way. No. This was *tink, tink, tink*.
We'd have made a day of it—searching
for the boy who made the sound. For he was us:
the young boy tinkering with the watermill,
perfecting the hit of hammer, each wheel's
revolution, water tripping a hollow music
from a foot-wide rill swollen with melted snow.

*

Late last night, I heard a hound striking a line
Remember the night our hound left—
three times up the mountain, twice down.

Was it rabbit or fox? Next morning
before we broke camp, a lone mourning dove.
*Melodic,* I called it, *naïve,* you teased
as we set the Musketaquid into the river.
And when the hound was gone, what was it
we'd lost?
              The clear space between trees,
looking up through the heavens, the oars idle
between us, the white lilies nearly open.
*June,* you said, *earlier than usual.* After that
I tracked the blooms, John, each season, every one.

# Elegy for the Bay Horse

Yesterday the thin rabbit drew close, daft as
only a newborn can be. I thought of you choosing me.

The rabbit, too, bore a star—celestial swirl
of white cowlicked on his forehead.

You lifted your head from sheaves of hay,
swung toward our voices: clearance and a vow.

Three horses, but it was hardly a choice.
Slow day after day, we lunged you in the small ring.

The first canter, all resistance. You leapt the pasture gate
to say what you needed to say. What we didn't know

we intuited. That star or heart, no comet.
The going was inscribed. The gulls flying inland,

the sky clear as only after rain.

# Skating on the Concord with Henry Thoreau

This is where I look for you—
the swaying front fields and long stonewalls.

That's the quarter call from the hall as bread
cools in a bee-hived skep in the hearth.

Children asleep with cousins. A log drops
in the grate, a flame shivers like a topsail

and you slip through the battered blue door.
Your black skates dangle from knotted laces.

Henry's calling you down to the frozen river.
By the serpentine rock, you and Hawthorne

bend to lace skates. For every sound an echo.
This is the cold dark, these are the stars.

Henry's gone in a crack minute, angular, hawk-
wild, so long and low you swear he'll fall.

Nathaniel's upright, elegant, master of the long glide.
It's Henry you chase, Paul. Your blade's quick script

sheering ice. The Concord's wide and shallow,
a knock-solid freeze, nothing like the Charles—

those dark pockets near the Natick falls
where Charlie Humphries sank and John Hoagland

muscled him loose as you and Steven closed the gap.
Three abreast, the river widens, you all grasp wrists.

Henry, agile as a copper penny, shims a hard right
and it's crack-the-whip—you're the lash, brother,

crouched on your heels spinning, steadied by stars.

# Late May Cutting

The meadow's light is wider
after the bush-hog goes through.
Deer no longer leave their fawns
in whorls by the crabapple
and no one's running barefoot.
But something fattens here
in the changed light,
stubble tipped, shorn.
The thoroughbred and I
begin again.

# Notes

The definition of "Vert" is from the *OED*, *Webster's Unabridged*, and *Random House* dictionaries. "Vert," the poem, borrows from *OED* entries for "vert" and "vertigo."

The epigraphs come from Henry David Thoreau's *Walden*, and Eamon Grennan's "With Skeleton and Shoes."

"With Rocks and Stones and Trees" is from Wordsworth's "A Slumber Did My Spirit Seal."

"Dear Henry,": Italicized lines are an exact transcription from *The Letters of Ralph Waldo Emerson*, edited by Ralph R. Rusk.

"Saint-Gaudens' Diana-of-the-Crosswinds": Augustus Saint-Gaudens' weathervane stood atop the old Madison Square from 1892–1925. On the same square, at the old Madison Square Garden, Harry De Leyer and his horse "Snowman" high-jumped to fame. Years later my brother, Paul Calello, worked at Credit-Suisse, which is alongside the park. We frequently met, as he left work, at the statue of Admiral Farragut. This poem is the first of several place-based palimpsests.

"In a Hurry": The idea of *beauty oblique* is from Patrick Kavanagh: "Memorable beauty comes to us obliquely while we are going about our troubled business." With gratitude to Tyrone Guthrie for their well-stocked libraries.

"The Arrow of the Angel Had Gone Too Deep": borrows details from the US Forest Service on lichen—which is not a single organism—but a symbiosis between a fungus and an alga. The fungus cannot live alone; together they thrive. The title is from a letter by Ralph Waldo Emerson about his grievously ill brother.

"All This Water and Wind" is for Eleanor Wilner.

"Sheep and Angels": Augustus Saint-Gaudens carved two female figures, Courage and Loyalty, within a bas-relief of waves under the statue of Admiral Farragut in Madison Square Park.

"Landmark, Compass" the title alludes to Ed Yong's summary of the science of migration in *An Immense World*. For details on black-poll warbler migration—specifically, the phenomena that hatch-years make the journey on their own, following, perhaps memorizing the coast while adult birds leave later and fly a direct route—I am indebted to Lisa Kiziuk, director of Bird Conservation at Willistown Conservation Trust.

"Bloodroot" is an older forest species, in the northeast it emerges in March, nearly the same time that red-winged blackbirds return. Bloodroot bleeds a red sap.

"Marathon" engages with the epic of *Gilgamesh*, specifically the passage where Gilgamesh tries *to outrace the sun*. This artistic antecedent seems a good fit for writing about my brother given his boundless energy and perseverance as he continued thrive despite a dire diagnosis. The poem revises a well-known image from the *Aeneid*. It's worth noting that Paul ran and finished the Boston Marathon on April 15, 1974 at age 14 with his friend Steven. They'd begun this quest at 12 and 13—the third try was the charm.

"Wreck of the Jason": Samuel Evans was the sole survivor of the Cape Cod wreck of the Jason off Pamet River station on December 5, 1893. The epigraph is from the *Cape Cod Historical Almanac* by Donald G. Trayser.

"The Heavy Lift of Wings" is for Claudia Emerson.

"After Seeing the Irish Modern Dance Theatre's *Lear*": After John Scott's *Lear*, performed at the Tyrone Guthrie Centre in August of 2017. For Valda Setterfield who danced the part of Lear at Annaghmakerrig.

"Pilgrimage": The Old Manse is where Sophia Peabody and Nathanial Hawthorne began their marriage on grounds originally inhabited by the Nipmuc and Pennacook peoples. Some of these poems—based on historical Concord and associated with my brother—draw on the Old Manse, Thoreau's journals, and hikes with Robert Thorson and Peter Alden.

"In the Yellow House Attic": is written from the perspective of Henry's sister, Sophia Thoreau. Italicized lines are from *The Journal of Henry David Thoreau*, Feb 5, 1854.

"Slavery in Massachusetts": Information and phrases are adapted from *The Journal of Henry David Thoreau* and Thoreau's essay, "Slavery in Massachusetts."

"Every Living Thing": from Aldo Leopold's "Thinking Like a Mountain." The full line, in reference to the bawl of a dying wolf, reads: *Every living (and perhaps many a dead one as well) pays heed to that call.* The inversion of ship's bones and whale's timbers is from Thoreau's *Cape Cod*. The figure of the wind as lion's paw is from Elizabeth Bishop's line: "a track of big dog-prints (so big/ they were more like lion-prints)." My gratitude to Susanna Deitz for an invitation to see the room where Thoreau and Channing slept and to witness the effect as the interior shutter was slid shut.

"Sophia at the Window": The italicized lines are from Sophia and Nathanial Hawthorne, etched on the window's glass after her miscarriage. "A simple, low content" is a variant on Shakespeare's *As You Like It*; Orlando and Adam, exiled from the court, set off into Arden hoping to find "some settled low content." Wendell Berry

79

identifies that phrase and the harsh adversity experienced in the forest Arden as the baseline of the pastoral.

"Siblings Beyond the Concord and Merrimack": After his brother died, Henry carried on with John's botanical journal. The poem draws upon Geoffrey Wisner's *Thoreau's Wildflowers* for the dated blooming times of Concord wildflowers.

# Acknowledgments

Many thanks to the editors of the following publications where these poems first appeared, sometimes in different forms and with different titles.

*Academy of American Poets:* "Dear Henry," "If the Room Spoke Back," "Vert" rpt.

*32 Poems:* "The January Pear," "Like the First Horses"

*Birmingham Poetry Review:* "Horse at the Half-Door," "Like a Grove of Trees"

*Blackbird:* "Feeding the Hounds"

*The Common:* "Dear Hesiod"

*Commonweal:* "Anthropocene," "Wreck of the Jason," "Windy Room," "Every Living Thing"

*The Concord Saunterer:* "Siblings Beyond the Concord and Merrimack"

*The Gettysburg Review:* "If the Room Spoke Back," "Palimpsest," "Sophia Hawthorne at the Window"

*The Kenyon Review:* "The Arrow of the Angel Had Gone Too Deep," "Oster, Oxter"

*Kestrel:* "Wearing His Shoes," "Where the Harrier Flew"

*The Moth (UK):* "Skating on the Concord with Henry Thoreau"

*Oxford Poetry:* "When Orpheus Sang"

*Poetry Magazine:* "Vert"

*Southern Poetry Review:* "Dear Augustine"

*The Southern Review:* "Dear Henry," "Henry Beston at the Outermost House," "The Oldest Dream"

*SWWIM:* "Mycorrhizae"

*The Yale Review:* "After Seeing the Irish Modern Dance..." "Hurricane," "In a Hurry"

"Dear Augustine" (as "Red Rover") was selected as the winner of the Southern Poetry Review's Guy Owen Prize. "Diana-of-the-

Crosswinds" won the New England Poetry Club's Barbara Bradley Award and "Anthropocene" was awarded the Daniel Varoujan. Some of these poems appeared in a chapbook, *Never a Note Forfeit*, published by Seven Kitchens Press. Gratitude to editor Ron Mohring and to Betsy Sholl who chose it for the Keystone Prize.

*Vert* is in memory and honor of my brother, Paul Calello. Deep appreciation to my generous readers: Eleanor Wilner, Dean Rader, Catherine Prescott, Natalie Staples, Adrienne Perry, Emily Wolahan, and Claudia Emerson—who guided the book early on. My gratitude to Heather Hicks, Anna Moreland, Tom Smith, and to my Villanova students and colleagues. Thanks to Lisa Kiziuk and Fred de Long for abundant details about the natural world, and to Elisa Wiley for technological expertise. Gratitude to Thoreau Society scholars whose work nurtured the Thoreau poems. My thanks to the Community of Writers, Fine Arts Work Center, Sewanee Writers' Conference, Tyrone Guthrie Centre, Villanova University, and West Chester Poetry Conference for community, time, and financial support.

Love to Jane, Jin, David, James, and Peter, and to Dad, Mom, my sisters, uncle, all the cousins and close friends who are extended family. My love always and evermore to the home team, you keep me going. James, my love, you make anything possible.

# The Wisdom of Winter

REFLECTIONS FROM THE JOURNEY

Jackie K. Cooper

MERCER UNIVERSITY PRESS
*Macon, Georgia*

MUP/ P679

© 2023 by Mercer University Press
Published by Mercer University Press
1501 Mercer University Drive
Macon, Georgia 31207
All rights reserved

27 26 25 24 23     5 4 3 2 1

Books published by Mercer University Press are printed on acid-free
paper that meets the requirements of the American National
Standard for Information Sciences—Permanence of Paper for Printed
Library Materials.

Printed and bound in the United States.

This book is set in Adobe Garamond Pro.

Cover/jacket design by Burt&Burt.

ISBN    978-0-88146-907-3
Cataloging-in-Publication Data is available from the Library of Congress

For Judy Adair Roberts, my memory keeper.

*Remember that I love you.*

MERCER UNIVERSITY PRESS

*Endowed by*

TOM WATSON BROWN

*and*

THE WATSON-BROWN FOUNDATION, INC.

# Contents

## Acknowledgments

It is hard to write acknowledgments. Not that there are not many people to thank, but rather because of the fear of leaving someone out. I do want to say thanks to Marc Jolley and Marsha Luttrell of Mercer University Press. Lord knows this book would not have existed without you. You have been the wind beneath my wings and the noose around my neck. You just wouldn't give up, and for that I am so appreciative.

Gratitude must also flow to my fabulous three—Dale Cramer, Milam Propst, and the late, great Jackie White. These three were encouragers, sharers, and teachers. They saw one more book in me when I couldn't see it.

Then there is my lunch bunch: Bob, Robby, Joe, Jay, Wade, Chris, Charlie, and Ashley. They helped provide stories for this book even when they did not know they were doing that service. I also got inspiration from AG the Intern (Amber Garrett). She has been a close friend since the day I met her and has always encouraged me to write another book.

For my family, which starts with my wife, Terry; sons JJ and Sean; daughters-in-law Angela and Paula; and grandchildren Genna, Walker, Natalie, and Mei Mei: you are everything to me and always will be.

And for you, the readers: I hope you get some entertainment, some inspiration, as well as some hope and happiness. God bless you all.

## Foreword

In the year and a half that I've known Jackie Cooper, I've learned so much about myself. Weird thing to say—I know. But it's the truth.

I graduated college at the beginning of the COVID-19 pandemic. And although my losses were small compared to others, my time in college was cut short, I didn't get a formal graduation, I lost my dream internship, and I watched several people around me get sick. In many ways, this time period felt overwhelmingly like the abrupt end of so many good things. I was devastated that all of my big plans to go to Nashville and work in the music industry were taken away from me so suddenly. And there was nothing anyone could do. However, this was only the beginning of what I now think has changed the trajectory of my life.

On December 4, 2020, I received a Facebook message. I opened it and saw a faintly familiar name. A name that I remembered from my childhood church: Jackie Cooper. Or shall I say Jackie K. Cooper? Jackie had reached out to me asking for assistance in something new he wanted to try on his viral YouTube channel. He wanted to know if I would help him conduct Zoom interviews with some of his favorite authors. I enthusiastically accepted and our partnership was born. We spent a couple weeks filming his regular YouTube movie reviews and author interviews, and eventually Jackie asked me to step out from behind the camera and get in front of it. I was hesitant, thinking I could never "perform" well on camera. After a few "pleases" and "Oh, c'mon, you can do its," I reluctantly found myself in front of the camera.

Jackie and I thrived on camera together. There has never been a moment when we didn't know what to say or what to do next. We found a groove and stuck to it, highlighting new book releases, reliving Jackie's extraordinary past in the entertainment industry, and recommending the must-see movies of the week all on our little corner of Instagram and YouTube. Thanks to this unusual partnership, we have connected with people all over the world. We have thousands of virtual friends from Georgia to Australia—and it never would've happened if Jackie hadn't pushed me to explore my talents.

That's who Jackie is. He is someone who sees the potential in someone or something and refuses to let it pass on by. He's a creative, an encourager, and an optimist. He thinks outside the box and always pushes me to do the same.

Over the last two years, Jackie has told me more stories about his life than I can count, and each one he tells has a purpose. Some leave you feeling an emotion bigger than what you felt just moments before. Some make you feel like you were right there experiencing it with him in real time. And others might even change your perspective on life.

Each story invites you in, like sitting down for a cup of coffee on a Saturday morning to catch up with an old friend. The way he shares his experiences, his relationships, his ups and his downs, the friends he's made along the way, and the family that is oh-so important to him makes you feel like you've known Jackie forever. And in some ways, I do feel that way.

The age gap that we love to joke about might be large, but "it's never too late to make a new friend," as Jackie would say.

As I said, Jackie has taught me many things. But they're not only applicable to me. I want to share the goodness that Jackie has given me so that you might take it and run with it.

You are capable.
You are accomplished.
Choose a career you love.
It is never too late to try again.
Anticipation is wonderful. Expectations will kill you.

But what I admire most is how Jackie has managed to slow down and remember the intricacies of his life like a good book he's read over and over again. The good, the bad, the great, the ugly—he remembers it. He remembers it because he takes the time to embrace the moments, the people, and the seasons of life.

I hope one day I can look back over the seasons of my life fondly and purposefully, like Jackie has done. I hope to make the most of every situation and capitalize on all the potential. I hope I accomplish half of what Jackie has. But for now I'll just slow down and enjoy where I'm at. I think I've got some time.

—Amber Garrett

# Prologue

As I sit down at the computer to write what will be my eighth memoir, I wonder what on earth is possessing me to do such a thing. Haven't I said it all in my seven other books? I am amazed to find that I don't think I have.

I love to write and I love to tell stories. That has always been my way. I learned from a master craftsman of stories and that was my mother. From my earliest memories, I relive sitting at her feet as she told me story after story of her life growing up in Gadsden, Alabama. She told me wild and crazy stories about her many brothers and sisters and the adventures they had. Then she told me about her boyfriends and how she almost married this one and that one.

The most special story was when she told me about meeting the cute iceman who delivered ice to the house of her sister Myrtle and her husband, Frank. Mother had been visiting them and was getting over a forced breakup with a young man of whom her family did not approve. This man was planning to be a teacher, and when he and my mother broke up, he casually said, "Who knows, Virginia, I may someday teach your son."

Years later, my brother attended Furman University. One of his classes was taught by Dr. Frances Bonner. You guessed it. He was my mother's old boyfriend. When she died, he attended her funeral. I had never met him, but somehow when I saw him standing at a distance from where we gathered for the burial, I just knew it was him. I asked my father who he was, and he confirmed it was Frances Bonner.

These and a million other stories about my mother and father flood my mind, but I am also recalling stories from my high school days, my college days, and the days thereafter. I have always liked to talk, to engage in conversation and to share stories with those with whom I come in contact. I have amassed a treasure trove of these memories.

And so now the fun begins. I am starting the journey of another memoir. I will have lots of company as I go back in time. The joy of doing something like this is you are able to conjure up people who have already left this world. For a short time, I can live with them again as I place their stories into words.

Eight books, eight memoirs. The words are waiting to reach the pages. I am brimful as I recall the seasons of my life. Spring, summer, and fall have gone, and now there is only winter. Winter is the crowning season and where my wisdom lies.

Turn the page and start the journey with me one more time.

# Chapter 1

# The Four-F Club

In the words of Charles Dickens, it was the best of times, it was the worst of times. I had retired from my government job and was spending my life watching movies and reviewing them, reading books and reviewing them. I had enough money coming in from my government retirement to keep my wife and me off the street and in our family home. We enjoyed our children and grandchildren, our friends, and our church. But my left hip hurt.

When I say it hurt, I mean it hurt. And it had been hurting for a long time. At first, I had blamed it on the wallet I carried in my back left pocket. It was thick, not so much from money but from credit cards and other collectibles I had filed there. That had to be the reason my hip hurt. So, I had my wife get me a pocket-clip type of wallet that I carried in my front pocket. I just knew that would stop my hip from hurting. It didn't.

My wife said it was from lack of exercise. Everything bad that comes my way is because of two things, so she says. It is because I don't exercise and because I am heavy. Now she doesn't call me heavy, that is my term. Never does she say I am fat. She just says I am a bit overweight. Her rationale is that if I exercise, I will lose weight and my hip will stop hurting. I tried walking around the neighborhood and hated it. Not the neighborhood, the walking. And my hip still hurt.

I talked with my doctor about it, and he said he could refer me to a specialist. I put him off on that and decided my pain wasn't that bad. I told myself that for months and months while the pain got worse and worse. Finally, I had had enough and agreed to see the specialist. I had tried everything from acupuncture to physical therapy by then, and I was tired of being sick and tired.

When the doctor looked at the results of my x-rays, he said, "On a scale of 0 to 10, with 0 being the best and 10 being the worst, your left hip is a 10." As I sadly absorbed that fact, he quickly added, "Your right hip is also a 10."

So, on Monday, February 9, 2015, I had my left hip replaced. It was the first surgery I had had since I was seven years old when my tonsils and adenoids were removed. Was I scared to have the hip surgery? You betcha. I approached that date like it was my last one on earth. I thought about writing farewell letters to both my sons but decided that was too maudlin. Still, I did ask my youngest son to come to the hospital before the surgery and pray with me and his mother.

The surgery went great, and it seemed like minutes before I was awake and in the recovery room. I don't know what medicine they gave me, but I woke up chirping like a magpie. I quickly introduced myself to the person watching over me and everyone else within earshot. I just had to know all their names and then repeated them to my wife when I got to my room. I was hopped-up on something and ready to roar.

As soon as I got to my room, they brought me some Jell-O, which I sucked down in one large swallow. The nurse said

I seemed to tolerate that alright and did I want some real food. I said I did, and soon they came in with a plate of meat, vegetables, potatoes, and bread. Whoosh, it didn't last long either. I asked for more, please, in my best "Oliver" voice, but none was forthcoming.

For whatever reason, I remained in that edgy state all day. As the afternoon wore on, I told the nurse I was going to need something to make me sleep that night. She assured me she would get me something. She didn't. I asked her for the last time around 11 P.M., and she said it was too late to contact the doctor to get something prescribed. So, I spent the entire night wide awake. I read an entire book that night and saw the sun come up.

That morning, another doctor, not the surgeon, came in to check on me.

"How did you sleep?" were the first words out of his mouth.

"Not a wink," I answered, and then proceeded to tell about my plea for a sleeping pill that had fallen on deaf ears. He promised I would have something that night to help me sleep, and I did. He sent me Ambien. The nurse brought it to me around 9 P.M. I was sitting in a chair, as they had already had me up and moving about.

"I am going to give this to you now, but when you get to feeling sleepy, you need to move over into your bed," the nurse said, handing me the pill. Now, I had never taken Ambien, but I had heard about it and knew it was powerful stuff, so I insisted she help move me to the bed as soon as I took the pill. The last thing I remember about that night was my head touching the pillow.

Now, let's talk about Ambien. It did put me out, but my dreams were wild. That night I flew with the bat people all over Columbus, Georgia. They were some of the nicest people I ever met and had puffy cheeks and little bat ears. I wasn't a bat person, but I could keep up with them, and when we landed I tried to cover them all up in my bed. When my wife asked me what I was doing, I replied I couldn't get all the bat people covered. When they started to disappear, I hated to see them go.

Needless to say, I asked for a different type of sleep inducer for the next night. It was provided, and I got lots of rest and was soon feeling good enough to go home. On Wednesday, just two days after my surgery, I was back in Perry, Georgia. The physical rehab specialists at the hospital taught me how to go up the steps in my home. I easily made it up the stairs to our bedroom, which is on the second story of our home, but once I got up there, I stayed until the following Monday.

When word got out I was home, friends and family dropped by to see me, most bringing food with them. That is something I love about the South. If you want to tell someone you love them, are concerned about them, hope they are feeling better—nothing says it quite like a casserole or some other kind of dish. In the South, we speak with our food. And when I am not at the top of my game, nothing looks/smells/tastes better to me than food. I go by that old adage of feed a fever, feed a cold, feed whatever ails you. You can now understand why my wife says I am a bit overweight.

One friend came to see me and we had a serious talk about my hip, its replacement, and the fact my right hip was now hurting. He asked how I was standing up to all of this illness stuff. I replied I was handling it all with the "Four Fs: Faith, Family, Friends, and Food."

He opined, "That sounds like a club."

I agree and ask all of you to join me. Membership is free.

# Faith

I have been a Christian forever. Honestly, I cannot recall a time when I did not have a strong belief. When some have asked when I found my faith, I have responded that I think my faith found me. I came out of the womb an empty vessel, and my mother and father poured their faith into me.

We were a church-going family, which means we went to church on Sunday morning and Sunday night and prayer meetings on Wednesdays. We attended the First Baptist Church of Clinton, South Carolina, where the minister was the Reverend Joseph Darr. Brother Darr, as he was called by his congregation, was the only pastor I knew when I was growing up. He retired when I was off at college. He was a formal man, always dressed in a suit and tie. I never saw it, but legend had it that he mowed his lawn in a suit and tie.

Brother Darr was a hellfire and damnation preacher. He would rant and rave from the pulpit, and his face would get all red and mottled. "If you are killed in a car wreck going home from this service," he would loudly say, with eyes blazing, "will you end up in Heaven or Hell?"

I was pretty sure I was going to Heaven, since my mother had told me the age of accountability didn't start until I turned twelve. So, I figured I had a "Get out of Hell" free pass like the card in my Monopoly game. Still, I always felt a sense of relief when we turned into the driveway of our house on Holland Street after we had been to church.

When I turned twelve, I went forward and asked to be baptized. It wasn't that I had a spiritual epiphany or anything like that. I knew I believed in Jesus and God and wanted to make sure everybody else knew it too. After all, I was twelve and could be held accountable for my sins from that age on. Brother Darr beamed as he patted me on the back and presented me to the congregation, another soul saved from sin.

A few weeks later, when enough sinners had been saved to justify a baptism event, I made my way into the baptismal pool. Brother Darr was there in a choir robe and a shirt and tie under it. As I made my way down the steps towards him, I said, "This is a lot deeper than I thought it would be."

I didn't mean it sarcastically, and I didn't mean it to be disrespectful. The water in the pool just seemed deeper than I expected. I think Brother Darr thought I was not taking the whole rite seriously enough, however, because he quickly grabbed me, put his hand over my face, and squeezed my nose. Before I had time to think, he had bent me backwards and dipped me under the water. Without having had time to catch my breath, I gulped for air and got water in my throat, which resulted in my coming up gasping and coughing.

Brother Darr propelled me towards the steps, where I was grabbed by some member of the congregation who was assisting in the service. I was virtually lifted out of the water and up the steps. My sins had been left behind and I was a new person.

We went out to eat that night, which was something uncommon in my family. We went to Louie's Restaurant, and I got to order an open-faced roast beef sandwich. That was my favorite meal to order when we "went out to eat," and I love it to this day. It was my father, my mother, my brother, and me. We all bowed our heads, and my mother thanked God for the food and for bringing me home to Christ.

My mother was my strongest influence for Christianity. She was normal, not a zealot, and she lived her faith. She also knew how to relate to people, how to have a good time, and how to laugh at the problems of the world. She read her Bible a lot and told me her favorite verses. She admitted she had a temper, but only rarely did I see it escape. When she used profanity, she always spelled it out. She would turn to my father and say, "I don't give a d-a-m-n about that." Or she would say, "Oh, h-e-l-l" when something annoyed her.

My father was also religious, probably more traditionally religious than my mother. He was the one who wanted to be there when the church doors opened. He was also the one who helped manage the money of the church and helped take attendance. He liked the company of his male church friends, who back in the days of my youth ran the church.

We were a family that had evening devotions. Before my brother and I went to bed, the family would gather in my bedroom. My mother would read from the Bible, and then we would join hands and say our prayers. We took turns and usually my prayers and my father's prayers were brief. My brother's were a little longer and my mother's were very long. When I was nearing desperation that she would never finish, she would "bless the poor, the sick, and the unfortunate." I knew at that point she was ready to end, and she did. "Amen" soon followed.

So, there we were in our house on Holland Street, a family held together by love and faith. It was almost idyllic. And then my mother got sick.

## Nightmare on Holland Street

It was Christmas Day and I was thirteen years old. We were in the living room unwrapping presents. I looked over at my mother and her nose was bleeding. I told her about it, and she went into the bedroom and got some tissues. After blotting it for a few minutes, the bleeding stopped. After that, I forgot about it until a few days later when she mentioned she must have a sinus infection as her nose had been bleeding some more.

After a few more days, she felt a swelling on her neck. She went to the doctor and he said it was a lymph node. He gave her some antibiotics and said that should clear it up. It didn't, and after a few more weeks, he made her an appointment with a specialist in Greenville to have it biopsied.

I knew what a biopsy was. Don't ask me how I had learned about them, but somehow I had. My mother confirmed my worst fears when she told me we had to pray it wasn't cancer. I did as she said and prayed harder than I ever had in my lifetime. I bargained with God and I begged God. I said my prayer in every way I could frame it to make Him hear me.

My mother went up for the biopsy and it came back negative, after which the lymph node was removed. When she came home, she had a bandage on her neck but otherwise seemed fine. But shortly thereafter, the swelling was back. Our doctor sent her back to the specialist for another biopsy. This time it came back cancerous.

When she came back home after hearing the news, my mother looked at me and said, "I guess we didn't pray hard enough." I was horrified. It was all my fault, or so I thought. I was the one who hadn't prayed hard enough. I felt useless all through the ensuing months when they tried different treatments to no avail. She died in August, a month before I turned fifteen.

After my mother's death, I fell apart. My brother left for college in September, which meant it was just me and my father in the house. With my father working long hours, I was alone for much of the time. I became obsessed with the idea my mother was somehow going to contact me. The crazy thing was that I welcomed such a concept with one half of my brain, and I was totally scared by the idea with the other half.

She didn't contact me, but God did, and He did it by sending me a peace about all that happened. I began to realize my mother and I packed more living and communication into the few years we had than other people gained with their loved ones over a lifetime. My mother had loved me, taught me, held me with such completeness. It was as if she knew she had a limited period of time in which to get as much said and done as possible. God whispered all this in my ear and it really comforted me.

It also helped that I felt I had an extra special angel in Heaven. When I prayed, and I prayed often, I communicated with God but let my mother know I was also communicating with her. Now, I know this was just my feeling and not the philosophy of any renowned theologian—still, it helped me get through this tragic time.

The death of a loved one is a terrible, horrible thing. It can make you doubt your faith, or it can help you build on your faith. I was able to build on mine, and I think it was for purely selfish reasons. If I rejected all I had been taught and all that I had read, then death would be the end. I needed to know I would see my mother again. That knowledge enabled me to put one foot in front of the other and move on into my future. It might not be something that would work for everyone, but it certainly worked for me.

As the days passed, living became the norm again. It was an alternate universe of a sort without my mother there to guide me, but I became used to it, even if I was not entirely accepting of it. I began to pray again, not in a family circle, but in one-to-one communication with God. And I still blessed "the poor, the sick, and the unfortunate."

## Jesus, Take a Seat

Years later, after I had gotten married and had two sons, that's when my wife got sick. She had been pretty miserable with a cold and a hacking cough, but that wasn't what concerned me. It was the fact her lymph nodes were swollen on the side of her neck. These were the same nodes that had swollen up when my mother got sick.

I asked around about the best person to see her and examine those nodes, and the answer I got was Dr. Don Rhame in Macon, Georgia. Macon was only thirty minutes from Perry, where we lived, so it wasn't inconvenient for us to go there. The truly amazing thing was Don was from my hometown of Clinton, South Carolina, and had graduated from high school with my brother. He remembered all about my mother's illness and certainly appreciated my concerns.

Don advised that we have the lymph node removed as it had become clogged. He also could not guarantee it was not cancerous. It made me a wreck. I literally felt myself falling apart. I remember calling my father and stepmother on the phone and sobbing that I couldn't go through this again. And I honestly thought I couldn't. I don't know what I thought I would do. I certainly didn't consider suicide or anything rash like that, but I was at my wit's end.

It was my wife who got me through it. She stayed calm about the whole thing and told me it was going to be alright. She also explained that we believed in a God who could answer prayer and who would be with us no matter what happened. Slowly her faith spilled over into me.

The day of the surgery came, and it was successful in that the node was removed without incident. However, Don told me it would take a few days to get the report back as to whether or not it was malignant. Those were the longest days I ever endured. I couldn't believe it would take so long. I tried to maintain a strong composure for my wife, but inside I was falling apart one more time.

Every day I would drive to my job in Macon, praying unceasingly that it would not come back as cancerous. Eventually, I just began to talk to Jesus and explained my fears to Him. I can honestly tell you I could visualize him sitting in my car with me, and He gave me consolation. This went on until we got the call saying everything was benign.

My faith got me through this trying time. Prayer gave me strength and prayer gave me hope. I do not understand how anyone can go through something like this and not have a faith in God to help them find peace. Over the course of my life, I have faced deaths, sicknesses, disappointments, and a host of other things that laid me low. In each instance, it was faith that carried the day. Plus, I have heard from my friends how it carried them through dark times also.

# The Loss of Shame

At least once or twice a week, I have lunch with my friend Bob. We meet at a place in Warner Robins that I call "Charlie's." I call it this because the manager's name is Charlie, and one of the things I look forward to when we go there is talking with him. Charlie is one of those people who has seen and done it all, or he knows someone who has seen and done it all.

Recently when Charlie joined us at our table, he talked about his special-needs daughter. He complimented me on how terrific my son Sean and my daughter-in-law Paula are in the way they deal with special needs children. He also commented on how great it is that their children, Genna and Walker, also help out.

Charlie was referring to the softball team Sean and Paula coach that is made up of special-needs children. They have been coaching for several summers now, and it is something the entire family looks forward to. Sean says it is one of the bright spots of their year. They love the thrill the kids get out of being able to participate in a sporting activity.

When Charlie was talking with me about the team, he said something I consider profound: "You know, Jackie," he said, "these kids are not the ones with special needs. All they want is to be loved and to be happy. The rest of us, we are the ones with special needs. We need this and we need that. We could learn a lot from these 'special needs' kids."

Then he added, "I have learned so much about life through my daughter. She has made me see things differently. I will tell you this, she is the one who has taught me and not the other way around."

I learned a lot sitting at that table and talking with Charlie that day. But it wasn't the first time I had heard that lesson. I have another friend who has a special-needs child. He told me once, "Don't feel sorry for me because I have a special-needs child. You should envy me because of all the richness of life I get through her." Amen to that.

A few days later, I went to one of Charlie's stepdaughter Avery's ballgames. Charlie wasn't there, but his wife was. Sean and his kids were working with their team and having a great time. Paula wasn't there that day as she had a work commitment. It was a mild afternoon, and I had intended just to stay for a few minutes and then head home.

It didn't work out that way. Sean was jumping up and down and giving encouragement to each and every kid on his team. Genna was in charge of making sure each runner knew which way to run, and she did this by running alongside them and, in most cases, holding their hands. Walker was in charge of pushing a girl in a wheelchair from base to base.

All of the twenty-seven family members and friends on the sidelines were cheering for whichever child was at bat, and Sean would pitch over and over and over until the ball was hit strongly or barely tipped. Then it was chaos as everyone shouted, "Go! Go! Go!" And off the hitter would go, either alone or with Genna helping guide the way or with Walker pushing a wheelchair.

I couldn't shout, I couldn't holler, I couldn't do anything except let tears roll down my face. I was an emotional wreck. I have never been prouder of my son and my grandchildren than I was that day. I was never prouder of humanity as a whole as I was that day. You just cannot believe the emotional wallop of that scene and the joy I discovered. It was beautiful beyond words.

At our lunches, Bob usually brings Gene along. Gene is one of Bob's oldest friends. They have traveled the globe together. Gene is a retired attorney and Bob is a retired judge, so they have legal backgrounds they share. Gene also wants to write a book some day, so he and I have that to talk about.

A year ago, Gene had what we think was a stroke. I was never clear if it was or not. Anyway, he was driving at the time and he wrecked his car. No one else was involved. He was in the hospital for ages after the accident and then went to live in an assisted-living facility. Gene is single and neither of his sons live near him.

When he was in the assisted-living facility, Gene was miserable. He couldn't drive, and I think he just felt locked in. Bob regularly picked him up for lunch, bringing him to Charlie's every weekday, but on weekends, Gene had to eat the food at the facility. Finally, he convinced his doctor to let him move back into his own house, which is where he is as I write this.

Gene being alone in his own house is driving Bob and all of his friends (me included) crazy. He doesn't eat as much as he should, and a lot of times if you call him, he doesn't hear the phone. But what are the alternatives? He doesn't want to be in an assisted-living facility; he doesn't want to move in with his sons; he doesn't want to be a burden on anyone. He just wants to live his life as normally as possible, but his health is making that difficult.

Old age is a difficult thing to face, especially if you are alone. Friends and family can only do so much. I remember my father in his later years telling me I needed to move to Clinton. I would explain to him I had a job and couldn't uproot my family. I would then offer to move him and my stepmother to Perry. "Absolutely not!" he would say. "I have lived in Clinton all my life, and I am not about to leave here now." He never did, and I worried about him every day until he died.

Worry, concerns—they are a part of everyday life. Charlie tells us you have to be worried about everything when you run a restaurant. He said one of his main concerns is how people treat his waitstaff. He told us a story about a man coming into the restaurant a few days ago. He announced his arrival to the waitress by telling her the food had better be good because that was the only reason he came to this place.

Then he added menacingly, "And if it isn't, then I am going to take this (bleep) food and throw it in your face!" The waitress went straight to Charlie and reported it, and Charlie told the man to leave and not come back. But can you believe someone would be that rude in the first place?

A few days later, my wife and I were in another restaurant and got to talking with our waitress, and she began to tell horror stories about her worst customers. She said a very nice lady came in to eat. When she took her some breadsticks, the woman looked at them and said they were too hard. The waitress told us she took the lady eight different breadsticks trying to get them right.

On the eighth try, the woman took the breadstick and beat it into her bowl of soup saying "Too hard! Too hard!" The soup splashed all over the waitress, but the woman wasn't concerned at all. "You need to go hose yourself down," was her response.

You hear stories like this and you wonder what has happened to society. Has it always been this bad, or is this a new phenomenon of the modern age in which we live. I have my theory about what has happened, and I call it "The loss of shame." When people lost the ability to feel ashamed of their actions, things began to go downhill.

It used to be if people cursed in front of a mixed group, they would catch themselves and say, "Excuse my language" or just "Excuse me." Not the case now. Profanity is used casually in a million different ways. As a film critic, I go see all the movies basically that are released in a year. And over the past several years, I have seen the restrictions of what can be said and shown on film disappear.

If a movie isn't rated G, then the doors are pretty much open. This doesn't mean a PG is the same as a PG-13 or an R, but it does mean that some of the factors that used to prevent a movie from being rated PG in the past, such as profanity or violence, might just sneak in there now. And a PG-13 now includes what used to be part of an R rating. An R rating is what an NC-17 used to be, while the NC-17 has virtually slipped away into the netherworld.

Sometimes I have heard people say as they grow older that nothing surprises them anymore. Well, that is not the case with me. I am getting older and everything surprises me.

## Remembering Pat Conroy

Sometimes the person you feel close to is not a dear friend but a rare acquaintance. That sounds contradictory, but let me explain. I don't remember where or how, but one day I picked up Pat Conroy's *The Lords of Discipline*. I fell into that book like a diver into a pool of clear, cleansing water. I was totally immersed in it, and it virtually blotted out everything else around me.

I had always been a reader, but only a surface reader. I had never before been made aware of the power of words, the passion of story, and the depth of true talent. Pat Conroy spoke to me in the words of that book and made me want to learn how to do something akin to what he had done. He ignited the flame in me to write and fanned it to higher brightness as I read his book to the end.

Maybe it was because the story took place in South Carolina, where I lived. Maybe it was because the hero of the story was so conflicted about so many things. Or maybe it was the passion for life that poured from the pages and swept me up in a turbulent tale of right and wrong in a semi-segregated South.

From that point on, I was a Conroy fanatic. I read everything he wrote and did it more than once. His books struck a nerve, and I wondered what it would be like to actually meet and speak with Mr. Conroy. I could only dream we would meet and realize we were two kindred sons of the South. Then the conversations and the friendship would ensue. Yeah, sure. I realized these were only pipe dreams and would probably never occur.

As the years went by, I concentrated more on being a book critic than being a book writer. Still, even that was exciting, as I could imagine Pat Conroy being bowled over by the brilliance of my critiques of his wonderful books. It was after I had reviewed *Beach Music* and sent the review to Conroy's publisher that I received a note from Pat's father, Don Conroy. He told me how much he appreciated the review and that he was going to send it to Pat, who was living in Europe. The note was signed Don Conroy, and underneath he had added "The Great Santini." Now I was within six degrees of Pat Conroy: I had been acknowledged by his father.

Soon after that, I became aware of a writer named Cassandra King. She had written a book entitled *The Sunday Wife*, which was recommended to me for review. It was only after I had reviewed her novel that I discovered that Ms. King was also Mrs. Pat Conroy. Soon thereafter, I was invited to a book festival where Cassandra King was one of the prominent guest speakers. As I got to know Sandra as a person, I was bowled over by her down-to-earth personality. She was herself in whatever situation you encountered her, and the name of Pat Conroy rarely, if ever, came up in my conversations with her.

There was a time when we met again at the Amelia Island Book Festival. I had been invited to participate, as had Sandra. One of the big events of the weekend was a luncheon where each invited author would sit with a group of attendees. As I approached the building where the luncheon was to be held, I spotted Sandra and rushed over to greet her. I warmly embraced her, and as I did, she turned to the man who had walked up, and said, "Look, Pat, it's our Jackie." From my vantage point, I could see Pat Conroy's face, and what I read from his expression was "he may be your Jackie, but he is certainly not my Jackie."

I got to see Pat Conroy many more times during his lifetime, and I have many warm memories of those other times. They have helped blot out that recognition of his "not my Jackie" expression.

## Do You Miss the Me I Used to Be?

Every morning when I shave (and there are some mornings that I don't), I am faced with my face. There it is staring back at me in full detail. On this one particular morning, I began to do an analysis of how the years had affected me. That means I noticed the lack of hair on my head and that the color of the hair that was there was gray. I also noticed some definite bags under my eyes and something jowly looking hanging under my chin. And there were crinkly lines everywhere.

Now, this does not mean I was suddenly horrified by how old I looked, but I did notice that an aging progression had definitely begun. This aging made me suddenly remember how I had looked (in my mind) just a few short years ago and that recollection was of being definitely younger. And as I contemplated my face, I also began to realize I just didn't have the energy I once had.

I have always loved to drive. Just let me get in a car and go and I was a happy man. I have never understood people who hate to drive. Of course, I am glad that they don't like the driving experience, because when I get in a car I want to be in control. I am the designated driver any time and all the time.

Most of our long trips are to Apex, North Carolina, where my oldest son and his family live. It takes about eight and a half hours to get there, depending on traffic and how many times we stop along the way. Thinking back on the last trip, I realized that after we got home, I was bushed. It had been a rainy day and traffic had been heavy. It took it out of me. The me that used to be wouldn't have been tired, but this present-day me was.

This led me to ask my wife, "Do you miss the me I used to be?" She looked at me as if to ask "Huh?" Then she replied, "What have I always told you that I find most appealing in a man?" I knew the answer to that question, so I quickly responded, "His brain?"

"That's right," she said, and then she added, "and your intelligence is as sharp as ever."

"I look that old, huh," I said half-smiling. "You couldn't have added in that I still make your heart flutter and I have never looked so good?"

"That too," she smartly said. "Better than ever."

That ended the conversation with my wife, but the thought that I was not as young as I once was stayed on my mind. I began thinking back to the marathon of movies I once watched in one day in an Atlanta movie theater. I had gone to the first showing at noon and then proceeded to watch three more after that one. (I managed to cram a quick meal in after the first two.) Then I drove back to Perry and never thought about being tired.

One weekend, we went to Atlanta for the AJC Decatur Book Festival. I was moderating a panel at the Decatur Library, so we left home on Saturday morning around 10:30. We stopped on the way and ate lunch, arriving at the library around one in the afternoon. The Decatur Library has a parking deck, so I wasn't worried about parking, but when we got close to the library, we found that the streets had been closed for the festival.

We had to park about three blocks away and it was all uphill. We finally got to the building, and I was huffing and puffing. We had planned to go to some other locations before my panel started, but once I was in that library, I was in that library; I wasn't moving for anything.

We finished up around 4 P.M. and headed home. Well, we really headed for Macon. When we got there, we had an early dinner and then rushed over to a nearby movie theater. I had to review a movie for my TV show, which we were taping the next day. By the time the movie was over and we drove on to Perry, it was about 10 P.M. and I was dragging. And I drug all the next day.

In my younger days, this would not have fazed me. I could have done this and still been raring to go somewhere else. But it seems those days are gone. It takes me longer to get going and in shorter periods of time I tucker out.

# His Name Was Garry

Everyone deserves to be remembered. I don't mean just Hollywood celebrities or politicians or financial wizards. I mean everybody deserves to be remembered. Such as my friend Garry. Garry was a son, husband, father, and friend, and he was outstanding in all those respects. I knew him because he cut my hair. He also cut my wife's hair and she adored him. Nobody could cut and style her hair like he could, she said. Me, I was the person he talked into getting his hair dyed. I was doing some TV work at the time, and he thought I would look better with a little "color."

Every time I went to see Garry, he had the radio on and tuned to a gospel music station. He was a devout Christian who always referred to me as Brother in the way we had called people Brother in my Southern Baptist church growing up in South Carolina. I was comfortable with it but never called him Brother in return. It just wasn't me.

Garry was tall, well over six feet, which meant when he cut my hair he had to lean over. This constantly leaning for his customers caused him to have back problems. Eventually it reached the point where it was going to require surgery. This is not something he was looking forward to in any way.

The last time I saw Garry, I went in for him to cut my hair. He immediately began to talk about his upcoming surgery and wondered how it was going to affect his business. He knew he would have a lengthy recovery period during which he would not be able to stand, and he wondered if his customers would wait for him to be back in business. I tried to assure him they would, even though they might have to go elsewhere in the interim.

Then he began to wonder about whether or not he should close his office for that period. That caused him concern and frustration. We finally came up with an idea whereby he could use the additional room he had added on to his home for his mother when she was alive. That could become his "salon," and he could then go to his main house and rest between customers. That seemed to satisfy him.

As I was leaving, he turned to me and said, "You know, Brother, God sent you in here today. He meant for us to have this talk. It really meant a lot to me." I then left feeling pretty righteous that I had helped Garry out.

That weekend my wife and I went to North Carolina to visit with our eldest son and his family. We returned on Sunday night, and I immediately got on the internet to catch up. One of the first things I saw was Garry's obituary. He had killed himself. I was beyond shocked.

During the next few days, I tried to analyze in my mind what had driven him to do such a thing. I knew he had been depressed when we talked, but I thought he had felt better when we finished. But depression is an evil foe. It can surround us with hopelessness. I have talked with many people who suffer from depression, and they say it is like you are alone on an island and there is nobody and nothing there to bring you joy. All of your worst fears and worst thoughts surround you and choke you.

There was also the fact he was taking medications for his back pain. Who knows what the side effects of those medications were. We see all the labeling that describes horrible side effects. We look at them and then go on and take the medication trusting we will be okay.

In my Southern Baptist upbringing, I was told that suicide was an unforgivable sin. I used to believe that. I don't anymore. God's grace applies to us all, and it certainly applied to Garry. He had lived a good life and had done so much good for those around him. Plus, he met the basic requirement: he was a believer.

I miss Garry, and I wonder if I could have said more or done more. I'll never know. What I am sure of is that the darkness overwhelmed him and he felt he had no escape except for death. And in those final moments, he just wanted peace.

This man was a good son, a wonderful husband, a loving father, and a generous friend. People deserve to be remembered. His name was Garry.

# Chapter 2

## One of Our Own

We buried one of our own today. We buried a friend, and we buried a member of our Sunday school class. My wife and I belong to the Christadelphian class at Perry United Methodist Church. We have been members of the class for decades. It was one of the first things we did when we moved to Perry. I don't know if we found the class or if it found us, but we walked into the class one Sunday and we knew we were where we belonged.

Over the years, we have attended church there too. Sometimes weekly and sometimes sporadically, depending on the current preacher assigned there. But even when we weren't happy with the preacher, we were always happy with the Christadelphian Sunday School class. It is our "happy" place; a place where everybody knows our name—and cheers to you.

It is not an easy class to get into. We can be totally cliquish, and that is not something of which we are proud. It's just that so many of us have known each other for so long. We just gravitate to the people we know and leave the "strangers" to sink or swim. But our class can teach you determination and patience, because if you try hard enough and stay at it long enough, you will become a part of us by osmosis.

When our friend Larry was diagnosed with cancer, the class went into a state of shock. He was as young as any of us. He couldn't be that sick. But he was. In order to do something, the associate pastor was invited to our class to pray for Larry. The plus was that while he prayed over Larry and his wife, Linda, the entire class gathered around them and touched them. We don't usually do things like that at Perry Methodist, but this was the absolutely right thing for Larry and Linda and all the members of the class. It gave us solidarity.

Larry put up a good fight, and he had some moments of real joy and optimism over the years. The cancer had gone away, but then the cancer returned. The solidarity remained. Larry and Linda continued to come to Sunday school when they could, and the class prayed and prayed.

Today, my wife and I went to the funeral service at our church. It was a celebration of Larry's life. The eulogy by Larry's best friend was beautiful, as was the entire service. Larry was well remembered and well celebrated. I know he would have been pleased. The Christadelphian Sunday school class sat together as a group at the service. We were still united. We were there for one of our own.

When my wife and I were dating, she told me she could never live in a small town. She was from St. Petersburg, Florida, after all. Flash to the present, and you could not blast her out of our small town. It is where we raised our kids. It is where we made our friends. It is where we can sit in a church pew and say goodbye to one of us without regret.

President George H. W. Bush was also buried today. He was remembered as a kind man, a gracious friend, a loving husband, and a good father. Believe me, he had nothing on my friend Larry, who excelled at those traits as well.

I will miss Larry, but I will remember his kindness, his strength, and a million other things. Most of all, I will think of the example he set for us as grace under pressure. He was exceptional and he was one of us.

## Kissed by God

Several years ago, a friend of mine asked how my mother-in-law was doing. I replied she was now in a rehab facility after having undergone colon surgery and that if she continued to do as well as she was doing, she would be able to move into an assisted-living facility. My wife and her siblings had already found a place for her, so that is what was next on the horizon.

When asked her age, I replied she was ninety-four. She had children, grandchildren, and great-grandchildren. Up until last year, she lived alone and drove her car. To be able do all that to me is a remarkable life. My friend replied that indeed she had been kissed by God.

And, indeed, Mary Lou Millard was kissed by God. She had a decades-long marriage with a man who utterly adored her. She maintained good health for most of her later years. She lived to have not only grandchildren, but great-grandchildren. She died at age ninety-six, and, according to her faith, was rejoined with her beloved Joe in Heaven.

Kissed by God. I like that phrase. Hearing it caused me to reflect on my own life. When I was growing up, all I wanted from life was to have a family. I had lost my mother to cancer when I was fourteen, and it left me shattered. From that point on, my main desire in life was to find the person I was meant to love and have my own family. This did not happen until I was in my late twenties.

I also wanted to work at a job I enjoyed and at the same time support my family. I accomplished those goals fairly quickly. So, at a relatively early age, I could look at my life and say, "I am content." Everything that followed was additional blessings.

I have lived to see my two sons as adults with families of their own. I have lived to see four grandchildren. Has my life been perfect? The answer is no. But it has been close enough to perfect that I can say I, too, have been kissed by God.

God was with me when my mother died and I stumbled out of our house on Holland Street and made my way to the First Baptist Church of Clinton. There I knelt at the altar and sobbed my heart out. God was also with me when I made my way, years later, to the Millard home in St. Petersburg, Florida. I arrived to meet my blind date. I rarely took the chance on blind dates, but this time my brother and sister-in-law talked me into it. Boy, am I glad they did.

God was with me when I accepted an invitation from a friend to visit the First Methodist Church in Perry, Georgia. Terry and I found a home there, a community that included people who immediately became our best friends. We have been members there for almost fifty years.

God was also with me in Rocky Mount, North Carolina, when my son JJ arrived. Knowing that Terry and I had created something so special was a joy that almost overwhelmed me. God was with me again when my son Sean arrived at the hospital in Macon, Georgia. He, too, was special from the day he was born.

As I look back over my life, I do feel that God put his loving arms around us, kissed the tops of our heads. Why? I do not know. It was purely a gift.

## *Where Else Would We Be?*

Years ago, when we moved to Perry, Georgia, the Watsons were one of the first couples we met at Perry Methodist Church. Draper and Dawne were the golden couple. They had it all—looks, money, a great family. We were impressed. Our friendship was built on seeing each other at parties, seeing each other at church, and seeing each other around town. We were good friends but not overly close to each other.

Then we attended a Bible study at our church. Somewhere in that Bible study, we bonded as two couples. We connected spiritually, and our relationship was never the same again. The Watsons became special friends to us because of this, and also because they shared their daughter, Christen, with us. Draper and Dawne had two sons pretty much the same age as our two boys, and then later had a daughter, which we didn't.

They would let us keep Christen at our house if they were going out of town with their sons, and we loved having her visit. She was delightful then and has remained so all her life. We have loved her since the day she was born. I remember well one day when we were keeping Christen. Terry had a meeting that night and made me promise I would not surrender Christen to her parents until after she got home and got a chance to see her. Luckily, she got home before Draper and Dawne arrived, so I was saved from a standoff with the Watsons.

Dawne Watson was everything you could want in a friend. And top of that list was loyalty. If Dawne gave you her friendship, it was given with a lifetime guarantee. Through good times and bad times, happiness and sorrow, she was with you. And everything she did was washed in sincerity. It all came straight from her heart.

Dawne died much too early. It was a tragedy for all who knew her. She shined and she sparkled, and we all basked in her glow. She taught me the meaning of true friendship. It happened when our son JJ got married. The wedding was in North Carolina, and Draper and Dawne had planned to attend. Then Dawne found she was going to have a melanoma removed from her arm. She told me, and I told her not to drive to North Carolina. Stay home and take care of yourself, I advised.

The night before JJ's wedding, there was a knock on our hotel-room door. We opened it, and there stood Draper and Dawne. Her arm was bandaged, but she was there. I was stunned they had made the trip and didn't know what to say. Finally, I stammered out a question and I asked what they were doing there. She replied, "Where else would we be?"

"Where else would we be" became my mantra for friendship. I thought about it over and over when I would go out of my way to do something for a friend, or a friend would do that extra something for me. They are words to live by in so many ways. And they clearly defined the relationship we had with Draper and Dawne.

As I write this, it is the weekend when we will celebrate Christen's wedding. We will celebrate her, her new husband, her father, and her two brothers. And most assuredly, we will celebrate Dawne. We will make the trip to Atlanta for the celebration. We will embrace the family, and we will look towards Heaven and search out the brightest, most sparkling star. And we will say to her, where else would we be?

# Everybody Needs a Robby

Years ago when I was growing up in Clinton, South Carolina, I had some good days and I had some bad days. In the South, if you are male, you are expected to be good at sports. I wasn't. I could not throw a ball, hit a ball, pass a ball, or shoot a ball. You get the picture. Because of this skillessness, I came in for a fair amount of teasing. I wouldn't say I was bullied, but I was teased.

In my sixth-grade class was a guy named Robby. Robby was a year or two older than me and most of my classmates because he had been held back a year or more. He was more mature in his looks than we were and more muscular to boot. He always excelled at any athletic event in which we took part.

One day at recess, we had one of those choose-your-team moments, and I was the last one chosen. It happens. I guess I must have looked a little bit desolate as I played my safe position of right field (I had learned early on that this was where the fewest of hits were aimed). Anyway, after the game was over, Robby came up and started talking with me. He asked me if any of the other kids had said anything mean to me. I said no but he knew I meant yes. Then he added that if I ever needed anybody taken care of about that stuff to let him know.

Throughout my grammar school and high school career, I never felt the need to call on Robby, but it was nice to know I could if I needed to do so. It gave me a kind of confidence I otherwise wouldn't have had.

Later, after I had graduated from law school, was married, and in the Air Force JAG office, I met another Robbie. Well, his name was Roberto, but his friends called him "Robbie." I worked in the legal office and had been assigned to defend Robbie after he was arrested on a drug charge. Due to my amazing legal skills (and a certain amount of luck), I got him a not guilty verdict.

Robbie was ecstatic and marveled that I had cleared his record. After the case was over, I didn't see very much of him, but one day my wife did. She was at the commissary and met him in one of the aisles. She didn't know who he was, but he knew who she was. He introduced himself and told her how her amazing husband had gotten him cleared in court.

Then, before leaving, he turned to her and said he was in my debt. And that if she ever needed anything to just ask him. He assured her she did not have to worry about anybody messing with her. Then he was gone. Though he had offered her protection, I think he scared her to death. Needless to say, we never needed to look Robbie up.

Now I am older and I have a good friend named Robby. Robby is a jack of all trades and a master of all of them. He can do anything you might need him to do. He has several business interests that involve wheelings and dealings that I can't begin to understand. I know he has several rental houses, and he is constantly repairing and refurbishing them.

Every once in a while, Robby will tell me stories about his adventures. He will talk about going into certain neighborhoods that he assures me I don't want to go into. Or about dealing with certain individuals he assures me I don't want to deal with in any way. When I ask for more details or when I ask why he puts himself in these situations, he replies that he does it so I don't have to. In other words, he keeps me protected from certain places and certain situations.

Now, whether Robby protects me from bad situations or not is a moot point, as I am not going to put myself in any situation that is dangerous. Still, it makes me feel better to know there is a Robby out there handling things that I don't want to be involved with.

So, I have had a lot of Robbys in my life. Some of them have gone by other names and have fulfilled other needs. Probably you have had some Robbys in your life too. I hope you have. And maybe all of us should reach inside ourselves and pull out our inner Robbys. We can be protective, or supportive, or just available. The world is a mess these days, and all of us need all the help we can get. So, if you see someone who needs a Robby, be a Robby for them. It will make the world a better place.

## On the Edge of Eighty

It dawned on me a few days ago that I am standing on the edge of eighty. Yes, that age of life that used to be so far away from me is about to come crashing home. Years ago, I remember hearing about the artist Grandma Moses. She was in her eighties when her artistic talent came to fruition. I found myself thinking it was amazing that she could still walk and talk at that age, much less paint. Well, let me tell you, I can still basically walk—okay, with a bit of a wobble—and talk, and I plan to continue to do so for some time to come.

What has been interesting is the reaction people have had to the news that I am about to be an eighty-something person. The good guys say, "No, that can't be possible. You look and act so much younger." The bad guys say, "Yeah, I thought you were about that age." My reaction is I refuse to get pigeonholed by either comment. I am who I am, and it is what it is. After all, what is the alternative?

One thing about being on the edge of eighty is you have a lot of life to look back on. I analyze the grammar school me, the high school me, the college-age me. Watching these reflections of myself, I see an evolution into the person I am today.

I was not secure in myself in grammar school. I was not popular, in my mind, as evidenced by my almost always being the last one chosen for any team activity. But it didn't matter because I was so secure in my home life. I had a brother, father, aunts, uncles, and cousins who loved me, and I had a mother who adored me. I also had the neighborhood kids, who thought I was pretty great. Who cared what those kids at Florida Street School thought.

When I got to high school, it was a different story. My beloved mother had died, and I felt cast adrift. To add to my unease, my father had quickly remarried and had antagonized my mother's family and some of his own. He had definitely antagonized me. So, I actually became a drifter, floating from one person's home to the next. I lived the Tennessee Williams quote of "depend[ing] on the kindness of strangers."

I would get up each morning after my father and stepmother had gone to work and leave for school. I always stopped by a local store and got a Pepsi and pack of peanut butter crackers to eat. That was my breakfast all the way through high school, establishing a pattern for me that has been there all my life. Now, even though my wife offers me breakfast, I still opt for my ingrained meal, except now it is a Diet Coke or tomato juice I have, and not a Pepsi. I still eat peanut butter crackers.

After school I would return home and stay in my room until around six, when I would be summoned to supper. After eating, I would leave and go to some friend's house and stay there until ten. That is the time my father and stepmother went to bed, so it was safe for me to come home. Then I would go to bed, get up the next morning, and repeat my life. The "friends' houses" where I went were sometimes people I knew well and sometimes not, but they all shared the common traits of generosity and kindness.

Aside from this routine, high school was a good time. I still was insecure because I didn't play sports, but I could smile to myself because I dated the prettiest cheerleader in the school. She gave me a large degree of popularity I don't think I would have earned on my own. We were *the* couple, and I basked in the warmth it provided. Our relationship lasted into my college years, and when we broke up, the town of Clinton went into mourning. This was not the way it was supposed to be—but, looking back from the edge of eighty, I know it was how it had to be.

# *High School Confidential*

Do you ever wonder why the four years of high school are so important in one's life? Let's face it, four years is just four years. You will spend a much longer period of time in your career, hopefully your marriage, and a variety of other experiences. But those four high school years loom large in the thoughts of those of us who have passed through them, and loom even larger for those of you actually going through them.

When I talk to kids I know who are either high school students or recent graduates, they refer to it as the best of times and the worst of times, with emphasis on the worst. From what I gather, kids are just meaner to each other than they were when I was a student. Plus, they have social media at their disposal, where they can really let out their venom.

For me, high school was a good place because my home life was in such shambles. I didn't get along with my stepmother, and so I fled my home as often as possible. High school was one of the places I found refuge. My teachers at Clinton High decided it would be to my advantage to graduate in three years rather than four, so they loaded me up with courses starting in the ninth grade so that by the end of my junior year, I would be set to take English in summer school and graduate.

I was already one of the youngest in my class, so that would have meant me graduating at sixteen. Everyone was fine with that, but on my way to my senior year, I decided this was stupid. I hung around and took my English class as a senior plus four electives. It was a great year.

The reason most kids don't like high school is they don't feel popular. One of the things I remember most from my high school days was that even the popular kids did not feel popular. I hung out with some of the most well-liked students in my school, and I know from experience they had their doubts.

Me, I never thought I was popular. How could I be? Clinton, South Carolina, in the fifties was a football town. I was not a football person. I did not own the highly desired "Block C" jacket. As a cheerleader, my girlfriend had been awarded her own "Block C," which earned me the opportunity to attend the illustrious "Block C Banquet." But did it make me feel good that I got to go? No. It just emphasized that I didn't have one of my own. Little wonder when I picked a college to attend it did not have a football team.

In my senior year, they had something called "senior superlatives." I don't know if schools still have them, but in my day, they were awarded in areas like "Best Looking," "Most Talented," and "Best Personality." They were voted on by the senior class. Some of my friends and I decided that if we wanted one of these "awards," we needed to let each other know what our priorities were. So, each of us agreed that when we voted, we would vote for the person who had picked that category. There were only about five of us, so there was certainly no guarantee.

Now, what was the category I would choose? I wasn't "Best Looking"—knew that. I could sing, but I didn't really consider that a talent like playing the piano, so "Most Talented" was out. And I certainly would not be voted "Best Athlete" by anyone. "Most Popular"—hah, I was more realistic than that. So, I decided on "Most Likely to Succeed." It had a nice ring to it, and I had been business manager of the school newspaper.

The first category for which we voted was "Most Popular." I could imagine who that would be as we had numerous people who were *the* most popular kids in my eyes. The next day when I settled into my homeroom, an announcement on the chalkboard said that a runoff would be held for most popular. It was Horace Payne versus me!!! Horace won and it was rightly deserved. He was a good guy then, and he is a good guy now. Me, I was in shock.

Now, I am not writing to brag about how popular Jackie Cooper was in high school. I am telling this story for all of those kids who don't think they are popular in high school. If you could really look inside the minds of your fellow students, you might find you are more popular than you could ever imagine. I always tried to be a nice guy, always tried to be friendly—it was just my nature. But popular, that was for those special kids in my class. At least that is the way I saw it.

So, keep on being you, the best you that you can be. You will never know what effect it is having on others.

By the way, I did get "Most Likely to Succeed."

## The Memory Keeper

As I teeter on the edge of eighty, I find myself gathering my memories about me. To do this, I rely upon the shared memories of those around me. My wife and children know me better than anyone, but they only know me from a certain age of my life. When I want to talk with someone who has known me almost from the beginning of my life, I turn to my friend Judy.

Judy Adair (now Roberts) and I became friends when my family built their house on Holland Street. Judy and her family were some of our new neighbors and welcomed us with open arms. It was my mother, father, brother, and me in our house. In her house it was her parents, Virginia and Grady, plus Judy and her sisters Linda, Sue, and Trudy. If you said the daughters' names from oldest to youngest, it was Linda, Judy, Sue, and Trudy. A perfect rhyme.

My birthday is in September, and Judy's is in January. I always break through those traumatic ages of fifty, sixty, seventy, and now eighty. She tags along a few months later. I think I was around three when we moved into the Holland Street house, so I have known Judy for most of my life. There were other kids who lived in the neighborhood. Mary Keith and June Adair lived next to Judy, and Maryann and Nancy Neighbors lived on the corner of Holland and Main Street.

Billy and Keith Trammel lived behind my house on Stonewall Street.

They were all great kids, but for me, there was no better friend than Judy. She was special from the day I met her. We didn't have a long time being neighbors, though, because while we were still in grammar school, her parents divorced and Judy moved away. But somehow that didn't affect our friendship. When she would come to visit her father, we would always pick up just where we left off.

Still, I have to admit there were periods of time when we were not in contact. However, I managed to keep up on her because her aunt married my father. I learned about Judy's eventual marriage to a great person named William, and I also knew when they had both of their daughters. I am sure she kept up with me and my life too.

With my father having married into the Adair family, my wife and I sometimes attended Adair family gatherings, which is how Judy and my wife, Terry, became friends and how I got to know William better.

Both William and Terry knew there was something special about the bond between Judy and me and encouraged it.

It was many years ago, blurred in my memory, that Judy and I began to call each other on our birthdays. We would have these fantastic conversations about life on Holland Street, and she would help me remember things that happened there. As she now says, it was the best of times, it was the worst of times.

We would talk, and I began to realize that she is my memory keeper. She knew both of my parents, my brother, and the child that was Jackie K. Cooper. She knew the day-to-day me. And I know those things about her. I have said many, many times in my life that everybody should have a "Judy" in their lives. She is the kind of friend you only find rarely, and the kind of friend that lasts forever.

Lately, we have begun to talk on the phone more often. Yes, we could text or we could e-mail, but hearing her voice is better. Just knowing she is there is a comfort to me. And when we get ready to end a conversation, she always says, "Remember, I love you," and I reply to her in the same way.

I hope everybody is lucky enough to have a "Judy" in their lives. We all need a friend who knows us, loves us, and accepts us; and we all need to have that special someone who is our "memory keeper."

## The Circle of Life

This past weekend, my wife, Terry, and I went to Florida for a memorial service for her mother, who died recently. We went with my son Sean and his wife, Paula. My son JJ drove down from North Carolina, so, for one of those rare times recently, we had both of our sons together with us. It was such a big thing for the four of us to be together again. Up till now, COVID had put any family-reunion plans on hold.

We had rooms at the same hotel on the same floor, so it was easy to move into one room to catch up. As I watched my two sons telling stories, I was immediately transported back to when they were much, much younger. They just lost twenty or thirty years right before my eyes. It is amazing how they still have the same traits, the same cadences to their voices, the same movements they had then. It was heartwarming to feel their closeness to each other and to us.

As the weekend played out, I became very aware how our relationship with the boys has changed. As we have always been protective parents—perhaps overprotective is the word—I now saw how protective they were of us. They were especially aware of their mother's needs and were right there with her at every move.

Also, for the first time, I literally did none of the driving. If we needed to go one place or another, one of the boys was there to take us. Now, it may be they just don't like the way I drive, but I think it was just making sure they could take care of us. My getting about is somewhat of a problem now, as I am a little wobbly on my feet and must use a cane for support. Therefore, they always drove up to the door of where we were going and let me get out before they went and parked the car. It was a little thing, but it meant a lot to me.

At another point, I was getting out of the car and my shoe came off. Before I could reach down for it, Sean was out of the car. He got the shoe and slid it back on my foot. This immediately reminded me of how JJ had such a hard time learning to lace up and tie his shoes and how many times we practiced it. Now here was my son putting my shoes on me.

Yes, the times they are a-changin'. I recall when the boys reached maturity I had a talk with each of them individually and told them how we were their safety net. Their mother and I were at the stage where we would no longer be their provider, but we would always be the safety net to catch them if they hit some difficulties. Now, as I look into the future, I see them as our safety net. I hope neither my wife nor I ever have to depend upon them for support, but I know they would come through if needed.

It isn't easy having circumstances change because of age. I still see myself as independent and in control of every situation, but it is a comfort having two people there if I need them. They grew up so fast. Like everyone says, it happens in the blink of an eye.

My wife and I raised two really fine young men. Yes, we are biased, but even considering that, they are still exceptional. They have been a joy to us from day one of their births. I love them both with all my heart, and, just as importantly, I like both of them. That is the secret sauce. They have always been people I enjoy being around.

So, as the years come and go, and the circle of life ebbs and flows, I am a happy, blessed man. I rest comfortably in the fact that should their mother or I ever need them, they will be there.

## The Friend of My Middle Age

Back when I was in my fifties, I was living the good life. I had just had my first book published, I was looking forward to retirement in a few years, and my kids were both in college. All was right with my world. I also had a large number of friends I had known for a very long time. So, in my mind I had enough friends, I didn't need any additional friends, I was too old to make new friends.

Then one night, I was asked to emcee an event at the Westfield Schools. I think it was a talent contest, but I am not sure. Anyway, I was standing backstage, and this other man was standing there too. He stuck out his hand and introduced himself to me as Arthur White. I had heard of Arthur before. He was in politics, had some kind of agricultural connection, and was a friend of Senator Sam Nunn. That was the extent of my knowledge, so I didn't think we had much in common.

But then he said the magic words, "I hear you like to read." I said I did and he responded he did too. He added he bought just about every book on the bestsellers lists, and he would be happy to share them with me. I eagerly agreed and asked for his address so I could drop by and pick them up. To my surprise, he said he lived about four blocks from me on Northside Drive. When he described his house, I knew exactly where it was, as I traveled down Northside about a million times a week getting to my house on Laurel.

And so began my friendship with Arthur White. He did own just about every book on the bestsellers lists, and, better still, he had read most of them and was eager to discuss them. I spent hours at Arthur's house sitting and talking books with him. It was fantastic. But what was even better was I grew to know Arthur's wife, Marge, and his kids, all of whom were delightful people. My wife became friends with Arthur also, and she thought the world of him.

At that time in his life, Arthur was having back problems. He had several operations while I knew him, but he always popped back. I can't tell you how many times I was driving down Northside, and there would be Arthur, out in his front yard, doing some kind of planting or some kind of something. I would pull into his driveway, and he would come over to the car and we would talk, or I would call and tell my wife I was at Arthur's and we would go into his house and talk.

Arthur and I didn't have a long span of time to be friends. His back problems and his overall health worsened, and eventually he died. One moment he was there, and the next moment he was gone—or so it seemed to me. It has been years now, but I still miss Arthur.

God used Arthur to teach me a valuable lesson. It is that you are never too old to make new friends. I always referred to Arthur as my midlife friend, and he thought that was funny. But he was. He became my friend when I thought I was too old to make any more friends, and when I thought I had enough friends. Boy, was I wrong. Arthur brought a lot of joy into my life, a lot of joy I otherwise would have missed.

Friendship is a gift, a gift to give and a gift to receive. I treasure my lifelong friends, but I also treasure my newfound friends. People come into our lives bringing different blessings, and some of them are unexpected. You don't want to miss out on any friendship that is offered, at least I don't. So, no matter what age you are, be open to friendship. You will be surprised how new friends, good friends can change and enrich your life.

## Going Viral

Three years ago, I went viral and I didn't even know what it meant. But hey, let's go back to the beginning. When I was little, my mother used to take me to the movies. She loved them, and she passed that love on to me. We went a couple of times a week because it was cheap entertainment. Plus, there would be one movie playing on Monday and Tuesday, another one on Wednesday, a new one on Thursday and Friday, and, finally, yet another a new one on Saturday.

As I got older, I made friends with Jimmy Young, whose father owned the local movie theater, and sometimes Jimmy and I would go there. There was something fantastical about being in a big building like that and having a huge screen where magical things happened. I felt at home there as I just let my mind be absorbed by whatever movie I was watching.

This love of/for the movies has lasted all my life, and at some point in my twenties, I became a movie critic. I certainly hadn't majored in film critique in college, so this was a case of loving something and just doing it. I watched a movie, wrote a review, and sent it to a newspaper. Surprise, surprise they ran it. And then I got more newspapers plus some TV review spots and I was off and running.

Eventually, I ended up on the internet. I can't remember going there, but somehow I stumbled upon YouTube. I started posting movie reviews and amassed a huge following of 136 people. You can't imagine how thrilling it was to know that a potential number of 136 people watched each and every new video I posted.

Then it happened. One Friday night, my son and grandson came over to my house and told me they had something to show me. I was interested in something I was watching and not really interested in what they had to show me. But they pulled up my YouTube channel and pointed out that my subscriber count had moved up from 136 to more than 700. It was like watching an odometer turn over as you traveled miles.

My son outlandishly predicted I would hit 20,000 by the end of the next day. We did that and more. By the end of the next few days, we topped out at 150,116. I swear, I thought it was a dream and it could not be real—or at least a bad joke someone was pulling on me. But it was true. I had gone "viral."

Finding out how this had happened was a real mystery, but we finally learned that someone had discovered my movie reviews and felt sorry for the old man who posted them so faithfully and only had 136 subscribers. He reposted on another site, and eventually my videos got the attention of "PewDiePie," a Swedish online content creator who has about a zillion followers. He gave me a "shout-out" and the rest is history.

I eventually found that the person who "discovered' me was a sixteen-year-old kid from Boston named Maxwell. He is one of the nicest people you would ever want to meet. He is in college now, but we stay in touch. I am forever thanking him, and I hope he knows how much he changed my life.

It was a life-changing thing in that it exposed my reviews to the world. I get comments from people in country after country, continent after continent. They write me encouraging words and during this age of COVID worry about my health. Many say I am like a grandfather to them. How great is that?! The amazing thing is this blessing is not something I ever dreamed about in my wildest imagination. It was not on my radar for things I wanted to achieve. It just happened (thanks to Maxwell).

Serendipities are what makes life so enjoyable. Somehow a sixteen-year-old boy came upon movie reviews made by a seventy-seven-year-old man and decided to expose them to a mass audience. He didn't know me. I didn't know him. But it happened just the same. If something that wild could happen to me, then just think what could happen to you. In one way or another you, too, could go viral!

# Chapter 3

## Routine Does Not Mean Rut

Some people I know fear getting in a rut. I fear getting out of one. I love doing the same things on the same days now and forever. I think this is why I don't like holidays. Holidays mess up routines. I don't like those days when the mail is not delivered and certain stores are closed. Give me the everyday, the sameaday.

It all goes back to the way I was raised. My daddy went to work at the same time each day; we had our meals at the same time each day. The mail was delivered at approximately the same time each day. I remember standing out in front of our house each day, Monday through Saturday, looking up the hill to get a glimpse of our mailman, J. D. McKee, headed my way. I usually had a glass of water waiting for him as our mail was delivered on foot.

Each day J. D. would pull out our mail from his bag and give it to me. Then he would look back in and say, "Well, look what they sent to you." It was usually an advertisement from the grocery store or a car dealership, something that everybody got. But when J. D. said it was for me, I thought it was for me. Do you know how special that can make a child feel? It was awesome.

Going to school was never a problem for me because school operated on a very strict schedule. You knew where you were supposed to be and when you were supposed to be there. To me, that was security, and security made me happy.

When my mother died, schedules went out the window. The world turned upside down, and I felt untethered from the earth. It was like I was in a pinball machine and was flipping from side to side, place to place. I longed for the security of routine, and I realized I would never have it again until I had a family of my own.

It took quite a few years before I found my wife and she and I had our family. But when it happened, it was everything I wanted it to be. We found our routine and our security. I like routine better than my wife does, but she accepts the fact I get joy from it. And that doesn't mean we don't have some spontaneous moments. After all, we did move to California back in the eighties, and I think that move shocked everybody.

In California we still stuck with a basic routine during the day, but at night we would sometimes take off for Los Angeles and go to a movie screening at a studio or at the Academy Awards screening theater. We sat in these places where the "stars" also went to view movies. Those were high times.

I have always said that all I ever wanted was a happy marriage and happy, healthy kids. God answered those prayers for me. But He also added on the movie-review career for me, and that was totally unexpected. The fact that it continues to this day is just the whipped cream and cherry on top of a life filled with happiness.

Even amid all this joy, I am still happiest with the routine of life. I love the people who are around me, and I love the things I do. I hope I can stick to the routine life has dealt me for many years to come. So, don't ever worry about me getting in a rut. I love the rut. Happiness is not tedious. At least, not for me.

What about you?

## *Love Thy Neighbor*

When I was a child growing up in Clinton, South Carolina, I knew all my neighbors and basically where everybody in town lived. In a town not up to 10,000 in population, it honestly felt that way. I knew everybody on my street and on the next street over and the one after that. I knew where everybody in my class lived and even where everybody in my brother's class lived. We were a small town, and we knew each other completely.

I hate to admit it, but as I grew older I was not as neighborly as I had been in the past. Of course, my wife and I knew where our friends lived and where our sons' friends lived, but when the boys left home, my wife and I pretty much stopped socializing in the neighborhood.

Those who know us know we are not yard people. We hire someone to cut the grass and trim the bushes. Plus, we do not have a great lawn. Our backyard is basically moss. Over the years, we have talked about having some trees removed and having the yard sodded, if that is a word. But no, we haven't gotten around to doing that yet.

When I leave my house, it is usually with a purpose. I have somewhere I have to be, and so I come out, get in my car, and go where I need to go. I do not come out just to breathe in the air and survey nature. If I am outside, I am going somewhere.

But we are still sociable. We do go to church and even occasionally a party. For example, a few months ago we went to a reception for a couple who had gotten married during COVID. Only close family attended the ceremony, and the couple didn't have a reception. They decided to get married, and then, when COVID had eased, to have their reception—which is what they did.

It was held outside and they served food. We were with our friends the Potts and were having a great time greeting friends. When it came time to eat, we got a table and settled in to enjoy the meal. A nice younger couple came by and asked if they could eat with us. "Of course," I said.

They sat down, and in my most oratorical voice, I said to them, "Let me introduce myself. I am Jackie K. Cooper. This is my wife, Terry, and these are our friends Bill and Susan Potts." The male member of the couple introduced himself and his wife to us.

Being Mr. Friendly, I asked if they had lived in Perry long. The female member of the couple responded, "Actually, Mr. Cooper, we are your next-door neighbors." She didn't mean down-the-street neighbors, she meant "go out your back door and look left and there is their house" neighbors.

It was honestly one of the most embarrassing moments of my life. I knew people lived in that house, but I had never gone over and introduced myself to them. And in my defense, I want to add that their driveway is on the other side of their house away from ours. Poor excuse, but better than none. Still, at that party, at that table, we had a wonderful time talking with them.

Sadly, I have not improved on my neighborly skills. I am still in my house most of the day most days. I go out to meet friends for lunch, and I do go to the post office to get my mail. But otherwise I still stay within the walls of my home.

Do I like my neighbors? I really do. And when they are outside and I am driving my car somewhere, I wave to them with enthusiasm. That has to count for something.

## Count Your Blessings

Lately, as I have been looking back over my life, I have realized that my life has been filled with answered prayers and blessings. Answered prayers are those things I prayed to God to give to me. Blessings are unexpected "miracles" that just happened and blessed me. I am sure you, too, can look back and see the answered prayers and blessings in your own life.

As my father got older, it was a struggle to help him out when he needed me. He lived in Clinton with his wife, Florence, and I lived in Perry, Georgia, with my wife and sons. I had a full-time job with the government and all the side work with my movie reviews I could handle. Still, I tried to call and visit as much as possible.

Many times when I was talking to him on the phone or visiting him, my father would tell me I ought to move back to Clinton. I would have to go through all the reasons why I couldn't move back to Clinton. Then I would add that he and Florence could move to Perry. To that he always gave me the "are you crazy?" look, which meant he was not going to budge from his hometown. I really can't blame him, as he had lived there for eighty-something years.

When we would go to Clinton, I always conducted a sort of ritual. I would ask about my relatives who still lived in the area. Then I would ask Florence about her relatives who lived in the area. Then I would start on questions about the neighbors and then move on to family friends. You can't imagine how much time you can spend just getting caught up. Daddy kept up with just about the whole town, so it kept my visits interesting. My wife, God love her, didn't know a third of the people we talked about, but she joined in when she could.

We always drove up on Saturday morning, took Daddy and Florence out to lunch, and then returned to Perry in the late afternoon. We never spent the night, and we never had a meal at their house during this time. When Florence and Daddy were both retired, she let us know she had retired from having overnight guests and cooking meals for company. These were the rules, and we abided by them, even though it meant an eight-hour trip in one day—four hours on the road there and four hours back.

During the year 2000, I was particularly busy at work. This was the Y2K-scare year, when all the computers in the world were going to collapse. It sounds stupid now, but at the time it was a real cause for alarm. We spent a lot of time backing up files in preparation for the possibility. And because of this, I didn't get to Clinton as often as I wanted. Still, Daddy was doing okay and didn't appear to have any major health problems.

In June, after a few weeks of not going to Clinton, I felt the urge to go. Something just kept nagging at me. I told Terry I was going to go. She asked me to wait a week as she was having some problems with her back and hated the thought of eight hours on the road. I agreed to wait, but on Friday I told her I was going without her as I just felt I needed to go to Clinton. She said she would go with me as her back was a little better.

So, on Saturday we headed to Clinton. Daddy and Florence looked good, and we had a nice visit, including going out for lunch. We also went through our usual liturgy of who was doing what. It was a very pleasant visit, uneventful in its sameness.

When it was time to leave, we hugged and kissed Daddy, and Florence walked us to the car. As she was telling us goodbye, Daddy hollered something from the den. Florence hollered back and asked him what he had said, and he hollered it again. We still couldn't determine what he was saying, so she went inside to see what he wanted. She came back out and said Daddy just wanted us to know how much he loved us. Hearing that, we got in the car and came home.

Three days later, he died peacefully watching TV as his beloved Braves started a game.

His last words were a blessing to me about his love. I hadn't prayed to God for that to happen, but I certainly did appreciate the blessing it gave me in my Daddy's words.

Have you ever heard the song that says "when I'm worried and I can't sleep, I count my blessings instead of sheep"? There is a lot of good, wise advice in those lyrics.

# Here Comes the Son

We were living in Rocky Mount, North Carolina, when my wife and I decided it was time to start our family. We had been married for a couple of years, and I was fast approaching thirty, so we thought it was time. It was another blessing from God that as soon as we decided to start our family, Terry got pregnant. We did not have the terrible problems so many couples have with conceiving.

I was employed as a real estate attorney for Hardee's Foods System at the time and had good health insurance. When we found out for sure Terry was pregnant, we made an agreement not to tell anybody for a while. But the next day when I went in to work, I think the first thing I said was, "Good morning, we're going to have a baby!" So much for silence.

We were just so excited. It was amazing we were going to have a baby. We talked about names. If it was a girl, I favored Virginia, for my mother. We would shorten it to Gena (to be pronounced Gin-a, which is what my mother was called). For a boy, Terry leaned toward Jackie Jr. I was against it. I had had a lifetime of people calling me Jack, and me telling them it was Jackie. My name on my birth certificate is Jackie Kershaw Cooper. It is not Jack and it is not John.

I tell people I was named for my uncle, and they assume his name was Jack. It wasn't. It was Aubrey, but for some unknown reason my mother and her siblings called him Jack. When I was born, they wanted to name me after him, so they named me Jackie. So, I am Jackie, named for my uncle Aubrey, who was called Jack. Complicated but true.

When it came time for us to go to the hospital, I took Terry in and was told to wait in the waiting room. This was in Rocky Mount, and at that time they did not allow fathers in the delivery room (God bless them). The waiting room I was in was across from the "baby room" so I could see all the other babies that had been born.

While I waited, there was a janitor mopping the floor. He was a really nice guy and we began a conversation. He asked if this was our first baby and I told him yes. He asked if I was nervous and I told him yes. We continued a back and forth, and then he disappeared through a door into the back of the hospital. He was back there a while, and then he came back into the waiting room and began to straighten up chairs.

In a few minutes, he turned to me and said, "That's a fine son you have." I quickly told him my baby had not been born yet. He replied, "Oh yes he has, and he is a fine boy."

It really kind of angered me that this stranger was trying to tell me he had seen my baby when I knew he hadn't. At this point, a nurse entered the baby room carrying a baby and brought it up to a circular hole in the window. "Mr. Cooper, come meet your son," she said, and pushed JJ's foot through the circular hole so I could touch him.

Meanwhile, the janitor was pounding me on the back saying, "I told you, you have a fine boy!" And I did. He was

JJ (the compromise Terry and I had settled upon) and he was named for me and my uncle Aubrey, known as Jack.

Terry's mother never could accept the fact we call him JJ. She asked for years when were we going to start calling him by his real name. Well, JJ is his real name and it fits him. He has done us and the name proud. Sometimes I do wonder what my life would have been like if I had been named Aubrey and he had been named AJ.

## If Not Now, When?

It was 1959 when I graduated high school. A large portion of the students I graduated with had been with me since kindergarten. We were a close-knit group, and I have stayed in touch with many of them over the years. Thanks to fellow student Jean Gettys, there is now a group of people in my class, as well as a few from other classes, who get together for lunch in Clinton every few months. My wife, Terry, and I have been back for one of these lunches, and it was great fun.

After each gathering, Jean sends out notes about who was there, what was discussed, and what news was uncovered. After the last meeting, she sent me a personal e-mail telling me about Julia, who was one of our classmates. She said Julia's health was not the best and she thought Julia might enjoy hearing from me. In her message, she included Julia's cell phone number.

Julia and I had been good friends in school, especially high school, but I had not seen or spoken to her since we graduated. That meant our last contact had been sixty-two years ago. What would I say to span a sixty-two-year chasm of separation?! I decided not to call.

However, in the next few days, Julia kept popping up in my mind. She and I never dated, we were friends. Still, I think I had a bit of a crush on her because she was so different. Julia was too cool for school. She never seemed to have the teen anxiety and angst that the rest of us had. Her mother had been a librarian and her father a college professor, so I imagined them having these artistic discussions over the dinner table. Julia knowing stuff about books and art made her a unique creature in my mind—sort of like Clinton's version of Audrey Hepburn.

I remember endless afternoons sitting on her porch steps or in my car outside her house talking and talking and talking. In my mind's eye, it was always autumn because there were big trees in her front yard that always shed the most beautiful leaves in the fall. The ground would be covered in them, and it gave the whole house and yard a multicolored look.

After a few days, I asked myself a question I ask myself a lot since I turned eighty: if not now, when? I certainly couldn't wait another sixty-two years to seek her out. So, I picked up my cell phone and called. A woman answered. I asked if she was Julia, and she said yes. Then I said, "Julia, this is Jackie Cooper." She gave a little chuckle of delight, and we fell right into a conversation. We talked for almost an hour.

Julia caught me up on her college years, her marriage, the birth of her children and grandchildren, and also her career as a schoolteacher. She had taught French, which had been her major in college. Now, why didn't that surprise me? Julia would certainly pick something that distinct to teach. She also talked matter-of-factly about her health. She was Julia, and she was still fascinating.

The amazing thing was there was no awkwardness. It seemed like I had talked to her the week before and we were just catching up. Sixty-two years vanished in a flash or in a flurry of words. She was still Julia, and I was still Jackie. We live in different worlds now, but for that hour, we were suspended in time somewhere in Clinton, South Carolina.

When it came time to end the call, I told her I would keep checking up on her, and I will. She said she would like that. Then, after a quick "Love ya" and "Love ya too," it was over. But it is not over. I will check back on her and see how she is doing and also relive the past some more.

If there is someone in your life you have been missing and you would like to make contact with again, do it. If not now, when?

## For Mikey: Part 1

In 1967, I graduated from law school at the University of South Carolina in Columbia. I knew that after I graduated I would have three months to prepare to take the bar exam. Following the bar exam, and hopefully passing it, I would join the United States Air Force. This was during the height of the Vietnam War, and there was still a draft. I didn't want to be drafted, so I had already made arrangements to go into the Air Force as an attorney.

Shortly before I graduated, I got a call from my father asking me to come home. That was unusual, as my stepmother didn't like having me around. A request for me to come home was an oddity. But being a compliant son, I went home.

The reason I had been asked to come home was so my father could make a request on behalf of his sister Alma Ruth. She and her husband, Mike, lived in West Columbia. They were a wonderful couple who had lived in Bennettsville, South Carolina, for most of their married life. Mike was a coach, and their son Mikey was a star athlete both in Bennettsville and later at the University of South Carolina. He was so great a football player they had pictures of him on the walls at USC.

After Mikey graduated, he married a young woman named Mary Jo and had three children—Skey, Burke, and Mica. Sadly, Mikey's life was a short one. In his late twenties or early thirties, he became ill and died. It was a true tragedy for his immediate family and for Uncle Mike and Aunt Alma Ruth. He had been their only child, and they adored him.

When he was in the hospital in Columbia, Mikey had called me and asked if I would come to see him. I thought this a little strange because there was a ten-year or so age difference between us, and we had never been close. But I went. Mikey told me when I got to his room why he had asked me to come. He wanted to know how my mother had handled her battle with cancer. He wanted to know how long it was between diagnosis and death, and other details. It was a somber conversation.

Mikey died a week or so after my visit. A year later, I was graduating from law school, and that was when my father called me home. It seems his sister had called and told him that Mike was not doing well handling Mikey's death, and she was worried about him. She knew I was graduating from law school and that I would have to stay somewhere for the three months before I took the bar exam, so she asked my father to ask me to come live with her and my uncle Mike for those three months.

I was stunned. I had planned just to keep the apartment where I was living until I took the bar exam. I had also applied to be a substitute teacher at schools in the Columbia area. I had things pretty well planned out. Still, there was something in the offer that appealed to me. I didn't know my aunt and uncle that well, but what I did know I liked, espe-

cially Aunt Alma Ruth. She was funny and smart and socia-
ble. She was the bright star of my father's generation.

Now my uncle Mike was another story. He lived and
breathed sports (I didn't). After all, he had been a football
coach for a large period of his life. He also was not the most
talkative person, at least he never had been around me. Still,
he had a wry sense of humor and seemed to like me enough. I
was nothing like Mikey, but maybe that would be a good
thing. I certainly wouldn't be a constant reminder of his son.

So, I said yes and sat there while my father called his sis-
ter and relayed my answer. Her only question was when could
I move in. I said it would take me a week to notify my land-
lord and get things together for the move. My landlord was
going to redo the apartment, so my moving was good news to
him.

So, one week later, I showed up at Mike and Alma
Ruth's house and embarked upon three of the best months of
my life.

## For Mikey: Part 2

In my memory, Uncle Mike and Aunt Alma Ruth's house had a living room in front and the master bedroom to the right of it. There was a hall out of the living room with another bedroom to the left and a kitchen to the right. There was a bathroom at the end of the hall on the left. Now, this may be totally wrong, but this is how I recall it.

When I moved in, Aunt Alma Ruth met me at the door. Uncle Mike was at work. He was the headmaster of a school, and I don't recall what Alma Ruth did, but in my memory, they both had jobs. Once I was settled in my room, I followed Aunt Alma Ruth into the kitchen, where she offered me something to drink. I asked for a Coke, and she pointed to some bottles on the floor. She had obviously gotten that information in advance.

The next question was whether or not I was going to be home that night. I didn't have anything planned, so I said yes. She then asked if I played bridge. I said yes, since I had been playing since high school.

Aunt Alma Ruth explained she had a friend named Sara who was divorced and loved to play bridge. "We play just about every night if we can find a fourth," she said, while at the same time lighting up a cigarette. She and Uncle Mike both smoked.

She then asked what I wanted for dinner. I immediately began telling her how I didn't want to be any problem or cause any work on her part, but she cut me off. Waving her hands about, she smiled and said, "Oh, honey, I don't cook! We either order in or pick up. This is what I was talking about" And with her cigarette she pointed to the side of the refrigerator where there were numerous menus for meals or burgers or pizzas.

"What are you in the mood for tonight?" she asked. Easily we decided on pizza.

And that's how my life went for the next three months. I would let them know when I was going to be home, and we would pick a meal. We would eat early, and Sara would come over and we would play cards, eat snacks, and smoke. And when I say smoke, I mean *smoke*. I had started smoking my senior year in high school, but I was truly a novice until I moved in with them. They loved the taste of tobacco, and it was rare when they did not have a cigarette in their hands.

My brand of cigarettes was Winstons. Alma Ruth never said anything to me about it, but there was always a carton of Winstons on the counter in the kitchen. I removed one pack at a time. When I took out the last pack, a new carton would miraculously appear. Again, it was never mentioned, it was just there.

The same thing happened with breakfast. I just assumed I would scrounge my own, but the first morning after I moved in, there was a knock on my door and Uncle Mike said, "Hey, Bud, how many eggs do you want?" I answered two and started getting ready for the day. When I came into the kitchen, there was a plate with fried eggs, grits, and bacon plus orange juice and coffee. Uncle Mike was sitting at the table drinking coffee and reading the paper.

He prepared breakfast for me every morning I stayed there. He didn't eat, but he sat with me.

Sometimes we would talk a bit, but not always. Sometimes it was just enough to have the company. The funny thing is, I had never been a breakfast eater. All through high school, it was a soft drink and a pack of peanut butter and cheese crackers. I continued this trait in college even though breakfast was available at the dining hall. In law school, it was Coca-Cola and crackers.

But somehow I loved those breakfasts that Uncle Mike made. I looked forward to them and made myself available each and every morning. Alma Ruth told me during my stay that he had never done that before for anybody. "He just seems to like doing it for you, Jackie," she said.

Aunt Alma Ruth called me Jackie. Uncle Mike didn't. He called me "Bud" or "Cooper" or "Coop." Other people called Alma Ruth "Madam" and Mike "Hop." Don't ask me to explain why. But I never did. They were always Aunt Alma Ruth and Uncle Mike. We had our own special relationship, and those were the names we chose to use.

## For Mikey: Part 3

Those three months I lived with Uncle Mike and Aunt Alma Ruth were times of healing. I noticed Uncle Mike laughed a bit more, and that Aunt Alma Ruth did not seem as tense as she did at other times. It was a time for me to heal also. Through all the days since my mother died, I had been look-ing for a family. I didn't find it in my father's house, but I did find it, sporadically, with friends' families or with a certain relative or two.

But I had not felt I completely fit in anywhere until I moved in with the Caskeys. They were not people who hugged or said I love you to me. Instead, they made me feel wanted and loved by setting out the Cokes and the cigarettes, by providing me with a breakfast each and every morning, and most of all by including me in their lives.

And so it went breakfast, work, dinner, bridge—eat, deal, and smoke. It may not sound like much of a way of life to you, but for me it was heaven. We laughed so much during that time. Uncle Mike had a droll sense of humor, and he could say some of the funniest things in a sly, slow way that might take you a moment or two to catch on to what he had said. And for some reason, they thought I was hilarious. They would ask about my day substitute teaching and would smile and laugh over any humorous tale I had to tell.

Soon it was time for the dreaded bar exam. It was three solid days of essay questions. The "question" was a set of facts, and the answer was supposed to be which law applied and how, with cases cited to support your view. After each session, a friend of mine, who was very smart, would ask me if I recognized a certain case that was needed in each question. I never cited the cases he had. Generally, I picked a case I recalled and pulled the facts over to parse out how this case I knew could be related. Sometimes it was a real stretch.

Uncle Mike, having been a coach, made me think I might get a locker room speech from him about how to play the game. No. I said he was a man of few words, and each of the three days he said, "Good luck, Coop." That is all I wanted him to say and all I needed to hear him say. His three-word salute gave me validation.

I passed the bar exam on the first try. My friend with the case knowledge did not. I was so elated, because I honestly thought I had bombed it. I was also sad because this meant my time with Aunt Alma Ruth and Uncle Mike was ending. I now would be going into the air force.

There was no big scene as I left. Aunt Alma Ruth hugged me, and Uncle Mike shook my hand and gave me a punch on the shoulder. He also told me to take the cigarettes that were left in the carton with me.

As I drove to Clinton, a zillion thoughts ran through my mind. They were scattered here, there, and everywhere. In the end, they all ended up in that hospital room where I was called to visit with Mikey. I thought about it over and over. He and I did not know each other very well, and he was in a terrible situation with his illness. Still, he told me when I left that it had helped talking to me.

And maybe after my visit he got the idea I should spend time with his parents after he died. And maybe he told Aunt Alma Ruth that. And when I graduated from law school and had three months of free time, maybe Aunt Alma Ruth remembered his words. And I think that is when she approached my father and asked if I would stay with them.

All those months I had thought I was doing it for Alma Ruth and Mike, and I do think I helped them in some way. Still, I truly believe to this day I was doing it for Mikey.

## For Mikey: Postscript

I thought I was through with the "For Mikey" story, but I found I have some last bits of information to add. The preceding chapter takes up with me leaving Uncle Mike and Aunt Alma Ruth's house after successfully passing the South Carolina Bar Exam. This meant I was now ready to join the Air Force, which I had committed to do.

I spent the next few months in San Antonio, Texas, attending Officers Training School. After I survived that, I thought I would be headed to a job in the legal office at some base in the South (which had been my preference). I did head back to the South after being assigned to Robins Air Force Base in Georgia, but I had been assigned as a special agent in the Office of Special Investigations (OSI). Apparently, there was no room at the inn of the legal office, and I was told this was as close as they could get me to my career field.

All of my Air Force days were spent at Robins. I had two years with OSI and then I was transferred across the base to the legal office, where I spent another two years. During this period, I spent very little time going home to South Carolina, which meant I did not see much of Mike and Alma Ruth.

One day, my father called to tell me I needed to go to see Alma Ruth and Mike. He said Uncle Mike was ill and I should go. I didn't hesitate and headed for Columbia. I had called ahead and told Aunt Alma Ruth I was coming. That seemed to please her.

When I got to the house, my aunt met me at the door. We talked for a few minutes and she told me how much Uncle Mike loved me, reminding me all over again how he had never cooked breakfast for anyone else before, not her, not Mikey, nobody.

I then made my way to the bedroom where Uncle Mike was. He looked tired and thin. But he always was thin. He had aged a bit, but he still had that "Uncle Mike" look. He was propped up on pillows, and he gave me that head down but looking up look. I wish I could describe it better, but that is the way he looked at you.

There was a chair by the bed and I sat down in it. I began to tell him how much fun it had been living with him and Aunt Alma Ruth. After a few minutes, he joined in with some stories of his own. We talked for maybe fifteen minutes, and I could tell he was tiring, so I told him I had to go.

As I stood up to leave, he reached out and grabbed my wrist. "You take care of yourself, Coop," he said.

"You too, Uncle Mike," I answered. And then I left. Aunt Alma Ruth had tears in her eyes as she led me to the door. I told her I loved her and she gave me a hug.

It was a sad trip to Clinton. I knew Uncle Mike was dying, and I didn't even know why. I still don't know if it was his heart or something else.

He died about a week after I saw him. I honestly think he was ready. Not to leave Aunt Alma Ruth, never that. But he was tired. I think he just wanted to rest. And I know he was ready to see Mikey again.

I have had a lot of people come into my life over the years, and I have appreciated and loved them all. Mike and Alma Ruth are at the top of my list. They loved me and I loved them. And love is eternal.

## What If/If Not

Recently I was talking with someone who asked me if I had ever played the "What if?" game. He explained that it entailed going back over your life and reflecting on what would have happened if you had made a different choice at a crucial time in your life. You know, the old "road not taken" idea. He said he had several moments in his life that his choice could have taken him into another life altogether.

I pondered on that idea for several days and came up with the conclusion that I didn't have many, if any of those moments. I really, truly love the life I have, and I am a happy, happy man. I wish my mother had lived longer, but her illness was not a choice I could make. And after her death, I basically made all my own decisions without much input from anyone else.

My life has been a series of "If nots," not "What ifs." After my mother died, my school guidance counselor told me I should take an extra load of courses and graduate in the summer after my junior year. That way I could go off to college and escape the misery of my life with my stepmother. I went ahead and took the extra courses, but when it came time for summer school for my last English course, I said no.

I realized I was already one of the youngest people in my class and I would be starting college at sixteen. That didn't sound like such a good idea to me. Plus, I loved my class and had a lot of friends.

This "graduating early" thing would put me in college with a total group of strangers. I said no and started taking more control of my life.

There was also the early commitment I had made to go to law school. I was not one of those people who thought I could change the world through the court system. Instead, it seemed to be a good way to make a living. The truth is I could have ended that law school thing at any time. No one was holding a gun to my head and saying, "You must go to law school." I made the choice. I decided to go, and it is not a decision I regret. I may not have wanted to practice law all my life, but it sure gave me a good start on my career.

I can add to the list of "If nots" by citing the names of Bobby Branch and Millard Grimes. Bobby Branch was the publisher/editor of *The Houston Home Journal*. After reading something I had written, he offered me a chance to write a weekly column. I didn't seek him out, he sought me out. He asked me if I wanted to write a column, and I answered, "What kind?"

He said, and this is hard to believe, "Write about anything you want." Me being me, I chose movies. That is where "That's Entertainment" started. I wrote that movie column for years, and Bobby was supportive from day one and more. He eventually sold the paper to Millard Grimes, who was even more enthusiastic about my writing than Bobby. I thought my career as a columnist was over when Bobby told me he had sold the newspaper. But no, Millard not only kept me in *The Houston Home Journal* but also put me in the seven other papers he owned.

Again, I did not seek Millard out, he decided on his own to expand my readership. There was just something there that Millard liked, and he ran with it. He told me once that he read every word I wrote—and that was a lot. I have always loved to write, and when you turn me loose, I can turn out the product.

I could cite a lot of other examples of times when I decided my fate or someone blessed me with an opportunity. It didn't boil down to a "What if" situation, where I had to make a choice. It came down to an "If not," where I made the choice or the blessing just fell into my lap. I have been fortunate to have people come into my life who have brought blessing after blessing. And for that reason, I am a very happy man.

I did a radio show a few weeks ago. It was by phone. At the end of the show, the host and I said goodbye. I had my phone on speaker and heard the radio host say to someone, "He always seems so happy."

Then I heard another person say, "I bet he isn't."

But I am. I really, truly am.

# Chapter 4

## Home Is Where the Heart Is

After I finished law school, I joined the Air Force. This was in the late sixties when Vietnam was raging. The draft still existed, and I was one step ahead of it when I finished taking the South Carolina Bar Exam and was admitted to the bar there. I had hoped I would get a slot at a Judge Advocate General's (JAG) office but was told there were no slots available. The powers that be said I would get something close to it, and that turned out to be an assignment as a special agent with the Air Force Office of Special Investigation. That is how I ended up at Robins Air Force Base, in Warner Robins, Georgia.

I knew next to nothing about being a special agent, but luckily, I was soon sent to Washington, DC, for a three- to four-week training course on how to be one. This course landed me in Washington in December. The course ran until the first week of January, and we were given leave over Christmas. I had found an apartment in Warner Robins but did not want to spend Christmas in a place where I knew very few people and was not close to anyone I knew.

Not really wanting to go home to Clinton, but having no other choice I could think of, I called my father and asked if I could spend Christmas with him and his wife—my stepmother. There was a pause on the other end of the line. Then he told me he didn't think that was a good idea. He said Florence now preferred Christmas just to be the two of them. So maybe I should think about going to visit my brother, Tommy, in St. Petersburg.

That meant Tommy was the next person I called. He seemed a little stunned when I asked if I could come to St. Pete to stay with him for a few days over Christmas. He quickly replied that he didn't think that was a good idea at all. He and his wife and children had already made plans for Christmas activities and he didn't want to change them. This ticked me off and also put me at a loss for any other Christmas plans. I whiningly asked him where was I supposed to go. He answered with these words, which immediately burned into my brain: "You know, Jackie, Daddy and Florence have a home, Helen and I have a home, but you don't really have a home."

So, there I was in Washington, DC, with no place to call home. I phoned my cousin Pat, who lived in Fayetteville, North Carolina, and started relating my bad fate to her. Pat and I had always been close, even though she is a few years older than I. Her husband was in the army at that time, and they were stationed at Fort Bragg.

Before I had my story half told, Pat told me to come to Fayetteville. There was no hesitation, no stuttering, nothing but a clear invitation to spend the holidays with her and her family. I really had called her to complain about my family, but when she offered, I gladly accepted. In just a few days' time, I jumped in my car and headed to Pat's, where I had a wonderful Christmas filled with love and friendship.

At this age, I look back on that Christmas and understand better why there had been no room at any of the Cooper inns. My stepmother and I did not get along, and sometimes we didn't even pretend to like each other. This put my father in the middle of our spats. My being there would have ruined their Christmas, and I wouldn't have had a great time either.

My brother and his wife had three children and were very active in their church. My being with them would have meant rearranging some of their plans. Plus, they were not wealthy by any means, and it would have been costly to have me sitting at their table ready to wolf down any food in sight.

Still, it taught me a lesson. I needed—and wanted—a home of my own. I wanted to have a place where the welcome sign was always on the door and the lights were always shining.

Since that ill-fated Christmas, I have always made sure I had plans for the holidays—plans that put me somewhere I felt comfortable. I have now been married for more than fifty years, so I have not had to worry lately about making those kind of plans.

When people ask where we went for Christmas and I reply that we spent the holidays at home, you can believe I say it with pure happiness. Home is where your family is, where love abides, where you belong. It took me a while to find my spot, but once I did, I never wanted to be anywhere else.

## *Ordinary/Extraordinary*

When I was growing up in Clinton, South Carolina, I lived on Holland Street. It was a quiet place to live, and very few people moved in or out. Most of those who lived there had been there forever. But one day, our next-door neighbors moved out and a nice young couple moved in. They arrived at about the time my mother was dying of cancer.

The couple were Dot and Avery Smith, two of the nicest people you would ever want to know. They were like a 1950s sitcom couple. He was quiet and kind. She was vivacious and friendly. You could tell they adored their life together, and I immediately loved being around them.

What I liked most about spending time with the Smiths was that they treated me as an almost equal. I was fourteen or fifteen when we met, and I assumed they were much older than I because they were married and expecting their first child. I don't remember them talking much about my mother being sick, so, in a way, being in their home was a refuge for me. Everywhere else I went, it seemed it was all anyone talked about.

Avery was in charge of the school busses at my high school. Because they lived next door, I became interested in becoming a school bus driver. At that time in South Carolina, you could drive a school bus at sixteen. I talked to Avery about it, and he told me when the next class would be held to train drivers.

I attended that class, but I must not have paid enough attention. I flunked the driving test because I drove across some railroad tracks without opening the doors. As Avery explained to me later, that was an automatic failure. When he told me that, I responded I would rather not qualify as a bus driver than risk the life of a child. Yes, I actually said that to him. How dramatic could I get! It sounds pompous even today as I write these words.

The years passed and I went off to college. I learned that Dot and Avery had moved away from Holland Street. I saw them once or twice when I was home, but we lost that special friendship we had. That is until May 2020. I was corresponding with someone from Clinton on Facebook, and for some reason I asked about Dot and Avery Smith. I was told that Dot was on Facebook, so I looked her up and contacted her. Dot replied, and we have carried on Facebook correspondence since that time.

I didn't ever correspond with Avery. Dot is always the person who messages. I told her again when I sent my Christmas wishes to them how important they had been to me in my teenage life. Then last week she sent me a message saying Avery had died.

Like I stated, Avery was a kind and quiet man. I mean it in the nicest way possible when I say that to me, he was ordinary. He worked hard, loved his wife, was kind and friendly to me. Over the years, when I have thought of him, it has been because of the respect I had for him. He was never in a bad mood. I never saw him get angry. While my life was utter chaos at times, my friendship with Avery was a calming force.

I don't think he ever knew how much I appreciated his ordinariness, but I knew from being around him that I wanted to be that way in my life, too.

I looked up Avery's obituary online. When he died, he was eighty-seven, just seven years older than I. The fifteen-year-old Jackie had thought him so much older, but it was only seven years. Eighty-seven years on this planet. I am so glad I got to share some of them. Avery Smith had been a good friend to me. He was my ordinary friend who brought some calm to my life in an extraordinary way.

## It Makes Her Feel Good

One of the things I have worked hard on in my life is being charitable. I always wanted to be more giving to others, but it is something I have to work at. When I was growing up, my two best friends were Tommy and Tucker. We were really thick, but in one distinct way I was different than they were.

If we decided to go to a movie and Tommy was a quarter short of what he needed, Tucker would always hand him a quarter. Or if Tucker was a quarter short, then Tommy would do the same for him. And I knew they never expected to be paid back. If it came down to me being the only one with extra money, I would hand it over but always add, "You owe me!"

It was just the way things were. Tucker had the least money of the three of us, but he was always the most generous. Tommy was generous to his friends but not others. Tucker was generous to everyone. I did notice when I was the one short of money and Tommy handed over what I needed, he began to add, "You owe me!" Tucker never did that.

Through my life, I have found that there are people who would literally give you the shirt of their backs. My sister-in-law Louann is like that. My wife told me she cannot mention liking something Louann wears or owns, because if she does, Louann will say, "Here, take it!"

Louann is one of the most generous people I have ever met. Countless times we have been in Florida, where Louann and her husband, Alan, live. When we would be getting ready to head back to Perry, Terry would be packing her suitcase and find new items, which were gifts from Louann.

Recently, I posted on Facebook I could not find any Campbell's Tomato Juice in our local grocery store. I implored people to let me know if they saw any on the shelves in any store in middle Georgia. I eventually found a Kroger's in Warner Robins that had it. But before I could post my discovery, I got a message from my friend Leelee Lewis. She said she had ordered me a case from Amazon.

I wrote her back to say not to do it and to cancel the order. She said no. Then she messaged me when it came in and told me her husband, Bobby, would deliver it to me. I told her to at least let me pay for it, but she refused. She also said she was sending me a surprise.

When Bobby came by with the case of tomato juice, he also brought some pound cake Leelee had made as well as several slices of caramel cake she had purchased. I asked Bobby to at least let me pay for the tomato juice, but he shook his head. "It makes her happy," he said. And I knew when he said it, it was true. She is one of those people who loves giving to others.

As I said, I am a fair to moderate giver, and I am an even worse receiver. I never feel a simple thank you is enough. So, I stammer around and try to say something that conveys my appreciation. I rarely feel I am successful at doing that. But it was brought home to me when I got the tomato juice and cake that there are people who feel good when they are able to do something for someone else. To me that is the ultimate giver.

Isn't there a proverb or adage that says "It is more blessed to give than to receive"? I am going to start working on being that way. I want to get so good at giving that people will say about me, "It makes him feel good."

# You Gotta, Gotta Have Friends

Being a living human being is a complex thing. We all have our strengths and we all have our limitations. I suffer, to some degree, from insecurity. It has gotten milder as I have gotten older, but when I was small, it started. Although I had friends, I never was sure they would be there for me if I really needed them. Let me quickly state this was a self-imposed insecurity and was not caused by any actions by my friends and acquaintances.

When I was growing up, I never remember having a birthday party. It wasn't that my parents didn't offer me one, it is just that I didn't want to have one. I was content to just spend my special day with my mother, usually to the exclusion of my father and brother. One of my favorite birthday memories was when my mother asked me one year what I wanted to do for my birthday. She said I could do anything I wanted.

Now, a lot of kids would take that and go crazy. I didn't. I said I wanted us (my mother and I) to go to the movie (big surprise there). I picked the movie *Salome, Where She Danced* as the film I wanted to see. This movie came out in 1945, so this is my fourth birthday we are talking about. It was a Western, and I liked Westerns, so my choice was logical. It starred Yvonne De Carlo, a semi-successful actress who would later gain much more fame as Lily Munster in the TV series *The Munsters*.

After the movie, we went to Sadler Owens Pharmacy, and Mother said I could order anything I wanted. I knew what that would be and immediately said a grilled-cheese sandwich and a vanilla milkshake. And, yes, the pharmacy had a soda counter. It was the way things were back then.

I remember that as my favorite birthday celebration. Like I said, I didn't want a party with friends. I always imagined that the horrible would happen and no one would show up. This stayed with me even after I married and we had our sons. My wife, Terry, would plan big birthday parties for the boys, and I would always try to persuade her we should take them on a trip or something. I feared again that maybe no one would show up.

My insecurities came to fruition in 1980 when I accepted a job in California. At this time, I had been working in civilian personnel at Robins AFB for a few years, and two of my coworkers said they wanted to throw a going-away party for me. Insecurity again!!! I told them no, that wouldn't be necessary. Still, they persisted and insisted, so I finally agreed to a party at the officers' club on a specific date.

One of the party planners came to me a few days later and said she had canvassed people and that my preferred date was a good one. She said she thought we would have close to a hundred people there. I was stunned. I didn't even know we had that many people in the personnel office. It was overwhelming, and I was on a high from the thoughts of such a party.

But from there it all went downhill fast. In a few days, she was back and said we had had some cancellations. I think she said about fifteen people couldn't come. Well, that left eighty-five, and that is a lot, I thought. But then ten more dropped out, and then some more, and then some more until we were down to nine people who had definitely said they would come.

I was pathetic. All my worst fears had come true. I was having a party and no one was coming. As the night approached, I was actually sick to my stomach. People were going to try to act nice and all, but they would see what a paltry group of friends I actually had. My wife practically had to threaten me to get me out of the car and into the officers' club.

My two friends who had planned the party met us at the door. They escorted us to the back area, where the doors were closed, and stood back as I opened them and was immediately met with a resounding "Surprise!" There were friends everywhere. Some were even wearing costumes from my favorite TV shows and movies. It was amazing.

Everyone told me how much they had enjoyed pulling off the joke. They said I looked more and more pathetic as the days up to the party had passed. They really got me, but it was all worth it. It was a tremendous party and one I have treasured in my memory for years now.

Did I learn a lesson? Yes, I did. It is trust your friends. Rely on your friends. Love your friends. Don't let your insecurities rob you of the grand possibilities life has to offer. It has been more than forty years since that party, and I am still in touch with many of the people I knew at that time. They are still good friends to me. As the song says "You gotta, gotta have friends."

## Anticipation and Expectation

Over the course of my life, I have indulged in anticipation and expectation. It seems that from my first memories, I was always living my life in anticipation of the future. It seems to have been implanted in my DNA. When I discovered food, I anticipated the next time my mother would make spaghetti (my favorite). When I started going to the movies, I was usually more impressed by the previews than the actual movie I was seeing. They always looked so good in those trailers, and I would immediately start anticipating their release.

I anticipated the mail every day because you never know what is coming in the mail. It could be a million-dollar sweepstakes. It could be anything. I felt the same thing about the phone ringing. I would think up a million great things that could happen with just a phone call. I just loved the unknowingness of it all.

Where I messed up was when I began expecting things. I expected my mother to live to be a hundred. I expected my father not to remarry after my mother died. I expected law school to be easier than it was. And the list goes on. In many cases, it was a person who didn't live up to my expectations. I expect a lot from my friends. I know that. It is one of my flaws. I make a judgment about my friends and how they will act or should act. Then a situation comes along and they don't act like I think they should—and I am disappointed.

One of my worst examples of anticipation and expectation not working out occurred at Christmas when I was a kid. Each year, my mother would ask what I wanted Santa Claus to bring me. And each year, I gave the same answer, which was that I wanted a surprise. My mother prompted me to reveal what the surprise was because Santa Claus needed to know. But I always countered that Santa Claus would know since he knew everything.

Each Christmas, I would wake up, run into the living room, examine what was under the tree, and then announce I did not get my surprise. At that point, I would go back to bed grieving over my disappoint. Now, I don't think I had a clue as to what I wanted the surprise to be. I was just a bratty little kid in that respect who should have really gotten coal for Christmas.

What is really fantastic are the things you don't anticipate or expect. Those are the serendipities of life. I never anticipated or expected to write a personal column for a newspaper. Bobby Branch at *The Houston Home Journal* handed me that bonanza. He got me started writing about movies. Then I did start anticipating every new issue of the paper, because I liked seeing my name in print.

I also did not anticipate or expect my YouTube channel to blow up and go viral. I don't think I was even aware that something like that could happen. But a teenager in Boston named Maxwell bestowed that blessing on me. He didn't know me. He wasn't doing me a personal favor. He just saw an old guy who put up movie review after movie review and only had a few followers. Maxwell decided to correct that, and, boy, did he ever.

So, there have been those instances in my life when I didn't plan for something to happen and so I didn't get to anticipate it happening. But those occurrences are the exception to the rule. Generally, I plan for the future. I always have some idea or another of something I want to do. I plan them out as best I can, and then I anticipate to my heart's delight. Oh, how great it is going to be, I think. Oh, what fun I am going to have, I decide. Sometimes, what I expect does occur and sometimes it does not. You just take your chances, but the joy of anticipating usually outweighs even a disappointing outcome. However, in extreme circumstances, expectations dying on the vine can wipe you out.

I was discussing this one day with my friend Susan Potts. She handed me some advice I have not forgotten. She told me anticipation is fantastic but expectations are a killer. I live by that thought. I still tend to dream big, but I always know that the day of what I am expecting will occur. Odds are high hopes are met with low results. A risk you take.

Still, I leave you with this. Shoot for the stars and risk the disappointment. Nothing ventured, nothing gained. You can never succeed unless you try. All of this may sound, trite but I believe it with all my heart.

## Topic of Cancer

Cancer is something we do not want to talk about, hear about, or even think about. Still, the truth is that most of us have actually had cancer or know someone who has. It came into my life when I was twelve years old. It was Christmas Day, and my mother had a nosebleed. Later, she developed a swollen lymph node. She immediately went to the doctor and was sent to a specialist in Greenville, South Carolina. We lived in Clinton which was about forty miles away.

One of the first things the doctor did was a biopsy of the node on her neck. It came back benign. But she continued to have problems, so they did a second biopsy which came back positive for cancer. She then went to Duke to see the doctors there. This was back in the early fifties, and there was not a lot they could do, and she died a few years later.

I have spent my life hoping and praying cancer would be eradicated. It hasn't been. There has, however, been great progress in the treatment of this horrendous disease. Over the years, I have known many, many people who have been diagnosed with cancer and later achieved remission or were outright cured. This has come about through medicine or, in some instances, miracles.

In my mother's case, I prayed as hard as I could for a miracle, and when the first test came back benign, I thought my prayers had been answered. Then, when I learned of the second biopsy, I listened to my mother and prayed again. When it came back positive, she said she guessed we had not prayed hard enough. Do you know how much guilt that can put on a twelve-year-old?!

Now, I am over the guilt. Do I believe in the power of prayer? Yes, I do. Do I believe in miracles? Yes, I do. I also know that I end all of my prayers with "Thy will be done." If you pray that, you have to accept that. Life is not always what we choose it to be. You have to take the good with the bad.

I remember talking with a person a few years ago who had breast cancer. She told me the diagnosis was worse than the treatment. She told me how just hearing the word cancer sounded like a death sentence to her. To keep her sanity, she began to do her own research. She educated herself as much as possible, and with knowledge came hope. Now, almost three years later, she is doing fine. She and her doctors fought the battle and won.

Today, in 2022, I believe if my mother were alive and the age she had been in 1953, she would be triumphant in her battle against cancer. I think there has been that much medical progress. I think there are new developments every hour of every day. I think there are doctors here, in Europe, Africa, and all around the globe who are doing remarkable things.

I believe in God and in science. Some people say that is a contradiction, but I do not see it that way. I believe God created us and God guides us. He gives the intelligence to the doctors, and he uses people in so many different ways to make our lives better.

My core tenet of faith is hope. Faith makes me able to hope. And that is what I am thinking as I write this. To everyone, I say, DON'T GIVE UP HOPE! Anything can happen, even if it sounds impossible. But even better is the hope inspired by the things that are possible today.

My mother didn't intend to be mean when she said we didn't pray enough. It was just blurted out. Still, it has taken me a while to find peace with that, but I have. We pray for miracles, but we must also pray for acceptance. They have to go hand in hand.

## Forgive and Forget

Recently I binge-watched the second season of the Netflix series *Sweet Magnolias*. I enjoyed it very much, and I appreciated the theme running through it. Each of the storylines for the main three characters involved forgiveness. It was about forgiving others and forgiving one's self.

I have always had a problem with being forgiving. It takes a lot to make me mad, but when I feel I, or my family, has been personally offended, then it takes a long time, if ever, for me to get over it. I started being this way when I was growing up in Clinton, when I would get mad at somebody for something they did or said and then hold a grudge forever.

When I was a child, I would sometimes visit with some neighbors who lived near us. They were great. They didn't have children but liked children a lot. I spent many, many afternoons visiting with them, sitting on their porch swing and swinging to my heart's content. One summer, I didn't go over as much as usual because a new family had moved into the neighborhood, and they had a daughter. She and I became good friends and started spending our afternoons together.

In the meantime, the childless couple had bought a new car. I could see it from our house, and I really meant to go over and see it, but, again, I let time pass by. One day, the lady came over to our house. She seemed really ticked off at me (I was ten at the time). She told my mother that I hadn't been over to see their car because I was jealous that we didn't have a new car.

My mother, being polite, told her she was sure that was not the reason. But the lady repeated her claim that I was jealous. I don't know why she was so obsessed with the idea, but she was wrong. At that point, however, I didn't care. I never went over to see that car. I never went back to sit on their porch. I never went over to their house again period.

Later, after I had grown up and gotten married and had children, my feelings of protectiveness encompassed my wife and children. One of my oldest son JJ's teachers didn't treat him as I thought she should. I told my wife I was going to have a conference with her, but my wife did not think that was a good idea. So, I didn't. I think JJ also begged me not to talk with her. Still, it stayed with me, and all these years later, I still think about it.

Now, are grudge holding and being unforgiving good things? No, they are not. I am certainly not perfect and have had to ask for forgiveness from friends and relatives. I was very, very happy when I was forgiven. So, what is my problem? I honestly do not know.

I do know I start my prayers each night with a plea to God to make me a better person. I know I have faults, and being unforgiving is one of my worst. So, I pray and I try to do better.

But a quick note about my prayers. I have a list in my head of people I pray for. It is mostly family, but there are also friends who are going through rough times, and I have told them I would pray for them. If I tell you I will pray for you, then, by golly, I mean to pray for you. So, I go through this ritual. I ask to be better and then I pray God will keep my wife healthy, happy, and safe. Then I move on to more of my family and then my friends. The new special prayers are added at the end.

The problem is I sometimes fall asleep in the middle of my prayers. I will wake with a jerk and have to search back to where I was. And then on I go and hopefully finish up.

I hope you will pray for me. That you will pray I am a better person, and that I will let go of grudges and be forgiving. I was taught to forgive and forget. At my age, I am more likely to forget the problem than forgive it. But I am working on it.

## My Funny Valentine

Valentine's Day is supposedly the most romantic day of the year. It is when flowers, cards, and candy are handed over to that special person in your life. It is a tradition that is long standing and publicly enforced by makers of those products. Millions are spent to guilt millions into purchasing these love displays.

In my youth, it was easier. You bought a bag of valentines. There were fifty or more inside the bag, and you just wrote your name on all of them. You took them to school and handed them to all the girls in your class. Okay, maybe you did buy one bigger and better card that went to that someone special. If it was a good year, that someone special gave you a special card back.

It wasn't until you were in the seventh or eighth grade and were actually dating that someone special that you started handing over boxes of candy. That may sound young to some of you, but in South Carolina in my youth, you could get your driver's license at fourteen. So, you were dating.

After my wife and I got married (many years after the seventh grade), she asked me to write her a poem for Valentine's Day. At first I thought she was crazy, but then I actually got into it and composed a pretty good poem. I actually have a talent for making lines rhyme. I have continued the poetry for occasions even to this day.

About thirty years ago, a friend of mine fell in love with a very nice woman. He told me she was the one and that he planned to marry her. The problem was that she wanted some special romantic gesture from him. He said he had racked his brain as to what he could do. He had sent her flowers, he had given her candy, but that was in the past, and she still wanted something better. He was desperate for a great idea as to what he could do.

I suggested a poem. He grabbed on to that suggestion like a duck on a June bug. That was the answer. That was the solution. That was the problem. He had no talent for poetry. What he scribbled down day after day was pathetic. I knew it. He knew it. She would soon know it.

Now, have you ever heard of *Cyrano de Bergerac*? It is a play written by Edmond Rostand in the late years of the nineteenth century. It tells the story of a man named Cyrano de Bergerac, who has an enormous nose. He loves the fair Roxane but knows that she could never love him due to his face-dominating nose. So, they spend their days as friends until she one day spies a handsome man named Christian.

Christian has the looks but not the smarts. He realizes that he cannot pursue Roxane completely since he lacks the ability to eloquently express or write his feelings. What can he do? He can get his new friend Cyrano to feed him words to speak or even provide him with love letters that would make any woman fall in love. Which is what Roxane does.

My poem was worthy of being called Cyrano-ish. It was one of my best. I gave it to my friend, and he gave it to the woman he loved. Supposedly, she responded to the poem by saying if she had any doubts, she had none now. It sealed the deal. They have now been married for more than twenty years.

I wonder if he ever told her he was not the author of the poem. He never told me if he did or not. It doesn't matter. It was his poem, and he could do with it what he pleased. I did tell my wife about the poem. She said that was okay. I just had better not give any of the poems I wrote for her away. And I haven't.

Love is still in the air. Cupid is still flying around shooting love arrows into the hearts of many in order to bring on the love. But sometimes he needs a poem by a friend to get the job done.

## The Name Game

Does it matter what name you give your children? You betcha. As a man of some years who is named Jackie K. Cooper, it can take a while to come to terms with your name. People do not like it that a man is named "Jackie." Oh, they may accept it up till he hits his teens, but then the "ie" should be chopped off so he can be known thenceforth as Jack. The problem is my name isn't Jack, it is Jackie. Check my birth certificate and see for yourself. My parents named me J-A-C-K-I-E. That's the way you spell it, here's the way you yell it—JACKIE!!!

I was named after my uncle, one of my mother's brothers. Their names were Aubrey, Horace, Robert, and Jerry. So, how did Virginia Cooper squeeze Jackie out of that group of names? Pay close attention. My uncle Aubrey was nicknamed Jack for some lost-to-history reason. My mother adored her brother Aubrey, so she named me after his nickname. So, technically, I am named after my uncle Aubrey.

It really irked my father-in-law that I went by the name of Jackie. He never once called me that. He always called me Jack, and shortly thereafter you would hear my wife reminding him that my name was Jackie. I got used to it. Just like I got used to me introducing myself as Jackie Cooper and having the person I am meeting reply, "Nice to meet you, Jack."

Then there were the people who had actually heard of the famous child actor Jackie Cooper. I can't tell you how many times I have been asked if I was really in the "Little Rascals." I am old, but not that old. Jackie Cooper had a long career. As an adult, he was the lead actor in a show about a navy doctor called *Hennessey* and also starred in another series titled *The People's Choice*. In that one he had a dog named Cleo.

Many, many times I have been asked, "How's Cleo?"

Cooper's last big event as an actor was when he was cast as Perry White in the Christopher Reeve Superman series of movies. I have to say it was a little thrilling to see my name come crashing onto the movie screen. It was shortly after he starred in *Superman* that I was contacted by the team at *Password*. They wanted me to come on as the contestant and play with the real Jackie Cooper. I was game for it, but supposedly it never fit into his schedule.

Later, Mr. Cooper wrote his autobiography. It was titled *Please Don't Shoot My Dog*. It seems that whenever they wanted to get little Jackie to cry on camera, they would tell him they were going to shoot his dog if he didn't emote. I reviewed the book for *The Atlanta Journal*.

I used to collect "Jackie" names in order to defend my determination to stick with my given name. If someone said Jack and I corrected them, I would add, "As in Jackie Robinson, Jackie Gleason, Jackie Chan, Jackie Mason, Jackie Cooper, Jackie Coogan, etc." I was well prepared. As shared earlier, these experiences helped inform our decision to call our first child JJ rather than the name printed on his birth certificate—which is "Jackie Kershaw Cooper."

With that settled, we were well prepared for the name of our second son. When he arrived, we named him Sean Christopher Cooper. I was writing a column for the local newspaper at that time and devoted an entire column to his birth. It caused a lot of confusion as to how the name should be pronounced. I remember a friend of mine congratulating me on Sean's birth, but then adding, "But why did you name him See-Ann?" Had these people never heard of Sean Connery?!

So, mull over what you have read here and realize some names are good and some are not. It took me a while to embrace my inner Jackie, but now I wear it like a badge of honor.

Let's hear it for the Jackies!

## $4 Million Dollars!!!

Just about every day during the week, I head to my favorite local restaurant for lunch. There at the Oil Lamp are usually waiting two of my best friends—Bob Richardson and Robby Russell. Bob is a retired judge and Robby is, well, Robby is Robby. He is forever asking me to ride around with him in his truck while he checks out his rental houses or some other task he has. I always decline, as Robby and I live in two different worlds. There is the bubble of life I live in on Laurel Drive, and there is everything else that is Robby's world.

But even though we live in different bubbles, I love hearing the tales of Robby's adventures. He always has a new story to tell of something that happened to him or could have happened to him. I file them all away in my head and sometimes use the information I have learned. And, oh, do I learn.

Recently, we were talking about people hiding money in their homes. This information didn't surprise me, as I have known people who keep a few hundred dollars hidden away for a rainy day, a natural disaster, or some other horrible occurrence. I used to do it myself, but with my memory not being as great as it once was, I can't trust myself to remember where I put it. So, now everything is in the bank.

I do remember when one of my uncles died his children found money behind pictures, behind books, behind anything that could be used as a hiding place. I don't know if they found it all or not, but they sure did look.

Still, Robby once told me the best story ever about hidden treasure. One day at the Oil Lamp, he pointed to a guy in the line and told me the man tore down houses for a living. He continued that the guy really liked his job but that he would never go under a house because he didn't like snakes. I could certainly understand that. I don't want to run into a snake anywhere, and specifically not under a house.

As the man got closer to us in the line, Robby motioned him over. He then asked him to tell me about the house he tore down and the surprise of what was in it. He seemed eager to tell the story, so I gave him my full attention. It seems he had been hired to raze the house of a man who had recently died. After just about everything had been smashed or crushed, the family appeared and told him to stop where he was.

It seems the surviving family members had been told, or remembered, that the deceased former homeowner hadn't liked banks. So, they now wanted to go through the house to see if he had left anything hidden inside. They went through every piece of that house and found a total of $4 million dollars. I was stunned. I hadn't expected that to be the kicker of the story. Both Robby and the guy said it was true.

Can you even imagine that happening? If it were me, I would be very, very happy, but I would also have chills that I came so close to losing all of it. Four million dollars stashed away like acorns in a squirrel's nest—that is the stuff of legends, or at least I consider it to be.

Like I said at the start, I love to visit Robby's world in the sense that he has more interesting friends and more interesting adventures than I tend to have. There isn't a meal that goes by that I don't learn about something I never heard of before.

Robby has had at least four million adventures of some type, one for every dollar those people found.

# Chapter 5

# CODA

Recently I watched a film titled *CODA*. It tells the story of a family in which the mother, father, and son are deaf. The daughter, the youngest child, is not. She acts as the interpreter for the family, a role that is forced upon her since she's the "child of deaf adults." It is a beautifully made movie that takes the viewers into a world of which they know little.

The movie also served to make me think about the hearing people who are children of not deaf but non-hearing adults. Ask around, you will find there are many. I know when my mother died, my father became deaf in some ways. Now, let me quickly say my father was a good man, a kind man, a man who never meant to hurt me in any way. But my father was not psychologically prepared to be the sole parent of a teenager. My mother had always done the majority of the parenting in our house while my father made a living to support us.

I remember shortly after my mother died, and I had gone to school for my sophomore year, something was said or done to me that hurt. I waited for my father to get home that night so I could tell him about it and for him to tell me what to do about it. As I started to talk, he interrupted and asked that I not tell him as it would give him a headache. Later in life I learned my father had an unusually high threshold for pain.

He never had a headache in his life. What he had was a fear of giving the wrong advice.

Later, after he married my stepmother, there were times I felt I was screaming my head off but no one could hear me. That is not a great way to feel. However, I did find out I was not alone. I talked to some of my contemporaries, who told me they were in the same situation—CODA (children of deaf adults).

What is it about communication that is so difficult? It is all in the mindset. I have talked to adults about their children. They tell me they have gotten to the point that if someone wants to tell them something negative about their children and their actions, they don't want to hear it. They feel unable to take on another problem. They have become deaf.

I have found it in my own family from time to time. I think I am speaking English but the person I am talking to is speaking in a language I don't understand. The words come out of my mouth, go towards the person, and then fall to the earth unheard. There is no communication. There is no understanding.

Then there is the joy of having someone in your life who does communicate, does understand. My wife is that person for me. She gets me. She hears my words both of joy or sadness. We speak in a form of shorthand, almost knowing what we are going to say before we say it. What a blessing that is, and how wonderful it would be if I could have that communication relationship with everyone in my life.

*CODA* made me think again about how I need to be a better communicator. I don't want my children to be CODA. I don't want my grandchildren to be GODA, I don't want my friends to be FODA. I have to get out of my head and into my words. Remember when your mother used to tell you to use your words? That is what we need to be teaching more and more today.

Everybody needs to feel they are being heard, no matter with whom they are conversing. Feeling unheard is frustrating, stupefying, disheartening, and a million other words. I am going to try to speak up. Maybe you want to think about doing the same thing.

## The Beauty of Coping

It seems like recently I've been seeing sickness and death all around me. Of course, we are just now, hopefully, coming off of a pandemic that affected so many people and families that I know. I lost young friends, old friends, and every age in between. Thank God my family was spared. Still, I look at people who have gone through, and are still going through, sickness and wonder how are they managing to stay sane.

Then I think back to when my mother was sick with cancer. Once diagnosed, she talked openly with me about her treatment and future. She did not hide the fact that she could die. I remember telling her I couldn't stand it if she did, that I wouldn't be able to get through it. She quietly told me that I would. She said God had given us coping skills. When I asked what coping meant, she replied that it was something in us that increased our tolerance level for fear, sadness, and other things we face in life.

Later, as her illness got worse, I would lie in bed and listen to her moans. I would wonder how my father was able to sleep through her pains. In truth, I resented him for it. It was only after she died that I realized he had to get his sleep because he had to get up the next day and go to work to keep providing for us. It was his ability to cope that allowed us to stay afloat during these times.

Coping doesn't mean that bad things don't happen or that when they do we aren't affected by them. It just means that we draw upon our coping abilities to tolerate those things that hurt us the most. These are the things we think will kill us, but somehow they don't. We manage to take one step after the other, one day after another, and eventually the things that have hurt us are just a dull pain and not an overwhelming ache.

Many times when I have needed to cope, I have prayed that God would change the circumstances in my life. Sometimes He answered my prayers in the way I wanted, but at other times, He would do so in a way I did not think was best. Still, that is one thing about getting older. You have a lot of years to look back on, and in hindsight, I can see that most of the times when my prayers were not answered in the way I wanted them to be, they were answered in the best way for me.

Over my life, there have been times when I've drawn upon my coping skills to get through hardships. And when I had to use them, I would think back to another bit of advice my mother gave me. She taught me the prayer that goes "God, grant me the serenity to accept the things I cannot change, courage to change the things I can, and wisdom to know the difference." She just taught me the prayer. Years later, I learned it is the mantra of Alcoholics Anonymous.

After my mother taught me the Serenity Prayer, as it is called, I would quote it to people. Sometimes they would look at me a little questioningly, as if wondering who in my family was an alcoholic. It wasn't until much later I learned its true origin, but its message is so good and so strengthening I use it as a prayer to this day.

We are all on a journey with our lives and we will all face hard times. Knowing we can cope is a great reassurance for most of us. It means we can get by. We cannot be erased from our being. We can use skills and people to get us through the rough times. That means a lot to me. And if you take an "O" out of my last name—as in, "Oh, Me!"—you will see that I am a Coper.

## The Customer Is Always Wrong

Everyone locally who knows me knows how much I love the Oil Lamp Restaurant in Perry. It is my "Cheers" because whenever I come through the doors, I feel like everybody knows my name. They will yell out, "Hey, Jackie!" or really, "Hey, Mr. Jackie!" (as I am of that age and older than anyone working there). Then, when I am going down the line to select my food, the person serving will ask if I want my extra gravy for the roast beef and if I want the green beans in a bowl or on the plate. Finally, when I get to the counter to pay, the waitress will come up and ask if I want her to carry my tray. These people care.

Recently, I was there having lunch when there was a little bit of commotion at the door. A woman was trying to get through the doorway with her walker, and her husband was trying to help. They got in, and the waitress told them to go ahead and be seated at a table nearby. Now, the Oil Lamp has a buffet and does not offer a menu. The waitress told this couple what was available that day, they made their selections, and then she went and got the food for them. These people care.

A few months ago, the Oil Lamp was closed for some reason, so my lunch friend and I went to another restaurant. I had been there before and had always gotten good food and good service. The same was true on this day up to a point. My friend and I met there at 11:30 and immediately gave our orders. At a little after noon, a friend of ours entered the restaurant and came over and joined us. Now, this restaurant has a rule that you cannot be seated until your entire party is ready to be seated. I guess in some people's eyes we violated this rule, even though we had asked the friend to meet us there but he had said he didn't think he could. We took that as a no.

The waitress came over and took his order, but then came back to our table to tell us that the next time we had an extra person joining us, we would have to wait to be seated. I tried to explain that we had not known for sure he was coming and had already ordered our food assuming he was not. She said she was just telling me the rules and that the next time we would have to wait. I asked to speak to the manager, whom I knew, but she said it was his day off and she did not offer anyone else. I felt like I was back in high school and had been sent to the principal's office to be reprimanded for some unknown offense. I just didn't get the logic in all this. If I was having a meal there and someone came in and I asked them to join me, would I be committing some kind of offense?

A few weeks after this incident, a new restaurant was opening in my town. The opening was announced on Facebook. I thought that was a smart idea as just about everybody reads Facebook at some point, and it is free advertising. But as I read the announcement, I was surprised. There was no mention of the menu and what would be offered. Instead, the focus was all on the rules. I would think you would lead with the positive and sneak the negatives into the middle.

I have never worked as a waiter. I am sure it is not an easy job. A friend of mine did work as a waiter at one of my favorite restaurants, Natalia's. I was telling him what a great dining experience it was for me and my wife every time we went. I also commented on how attentive and agreeable the waitstaff was there. He said they were trained when they were hired that the important part of their job was to satisfy the customer. No customer was to feel unwanted and certainly not rushed. He listed a few more of the requirements of the waitstaff. It all boiled down to that old cliché that has seemingly gone out of fashion—the customer is always right.

Lately, it seems when I go to a fast-food place or a fine-dining restaurant that doesn't appear to be the case. There are exceptions, such as the Oil Lamp, but on the whole, I feel I am treated like they are doing me a favor by providing me with food rather than them being appreciative of my choosing their establishment in which to eat.

I love eating out and there are still many good places to go. What I have to do is make sure I don't support the not-so-good ones.

# Saving a Life

Many years ago, I was invited to speak to a book club that was holding its luncheon in Marshallville. I did a lot of speaking of this type back then, and it was always fun to do. I really got to know the ladies of the various book clubs and/or social clubs, so I always looked forward to these events.

On this particular day, I gave my talk and then stood around to speak with different individuals who had questions about a certain book or just about books in general. One of the ladies who stayed to talk was someone I knew from Perry, who had brought a friend from Macon with her. As I left and started the drive back to Perry, I noticed they were in front of me.

It was a pretty, sunny day in middle Georgia, and I was feeling relaxed as I drove home. Keeping my eyes on the road, I noticed a pickup truck heading our way. It had an attached flatbed trailer of sorts on the back. As I watched, the trailer came loose from the truck and drifted into the opposite lane and headed straight for the car in front of me. The car swerved out of its way, but that caused it to go off the road and into a ditch.

I pulled over immediately and raced down to the car. The front doors would not open, and both women were unconscious. I could not get a response from either one. By this time, others had arrived to help, and somehow we got the back doors open and then the two women had to be pulled over the seats to get them out. Once they were out, they were taken by ambulance away from the scene, but, surprisingly, almost as soon as they left, the car exploded. There had been a fire burning beneath the car all along.

Having survived all this excitement, I got back in my car and headed home, driving extremely cautiously. As I thought back on the accident, I realized just how close those two ladies came to dying, and maybe some of those who tried to help. Just the thoughts gave me a few shivers.

A few days later, I got a call from the lady who had been driving the car. She thanked me profusely for saving her life, but I had been just one of a group who helped her get out safely. Nevertheless, she insisted it had been me and me alone. She then showed her sense of humor by adding that she believed in the Chinese saying that once you save someone's life then you are responsible for that life. Therefore, I was responsible for keeping her safe for the rest of her life. I agreed and told her I would make that one of my solemn duties, and then we both had a good laugh.

What was even funnier to me, though, was the fact she would call me from time to time and tell me she was going on vacation to somewhere like Arizona. She would always laugh and say she felt really secure driving there because she knew I would be in the car behind her looking out for her and keeping her safe. She made those calls to me for years, and I have to say that accident bonded us. She made quite a few trips and I always kept her in my prayers.

She is gone now and so I don't get those calls anymore. She died peacefully at a good age. When I learned that she had died, my mind flashed back to her last call. "Are you going to keep me safe?" she had asked, and I replied that I would. "Good," she answered, "now I can get on the road with no problems." I told her I would be in the car right behind her.

She was a very sweet lady and it was an honor to "keep her safe."

## Live Life in the Moment

When I was fresh out of law school, I went to work for a company as an attorney. I provided legal advice to a certain group of employees and performed other duties. This group that I advised had to take part in travel to conferences and other work-related trips. It was a complaint I heard about the most. These people didn't like leaving their spouses and children, but it was part of the job.

One day, I got a call at my office that I will remember till the day I die. I was told that one of the men in my group had gone to Texas for a conference. He arrived at the destination, checked in to his hotel room, had dinner with others, and then went back to his room. The next morning, he did not show up for the conference, and when someone went to check on him, they found him dead in his bed. I was told I needed to go with a preacher and his supervisor to notify his wife of his death.

I was stunned. I had not known this was part of the job but was assured by my supervisor that it was. The preacher and the supervisor came to my office, and we rode together to the deceased man's home. As soon as the wife answered the door in response to our knock, it seemed she knew. Her screams still ring in my ears, as does the sight of her crumpling to the floor.

We said all the "right things" and got some friends, neighbors, and relatives to be with her. She had two children who just seemed mystified by the whole thing. She kept telling me he couldn't have just died as she had talked with him the night before and he had seemed fine. And she kept saying how many plans they had for the future, so many plans.

The whole experience was horrific, and I am grateful that I have never been put in that position again. I did think that once I got back to my office I would never see this woman or her family again. But I did. A few weeks after her husband's death, this woman called my office and made an appointment to see me. She didn't give a reason but just said she wanted to talk with me. I assumed it was a legal question.

When she arrived, she came into my office and sat down. The first thing she did was thank me for my kindness on that horrible day. She said she felt I was the only one who actually sensed the pain of what was happening to her. Then she told me that she didn't think he just died. I tried to assure her that all the tests on him revealed he died of natural causes. She stopped me and said she thought he had been murdered. I could say I was surprised, but in truth I had thought it myself. How does someone that young and healthy just die?!

Once again, she asked me all the same questions about her husband's death. Who had discovered the body? Who had seen him the night before? Who decided that he had to go to this conference? Question after question after question with only the same answers to be given. I knew she wanted something more, but there just wasn't anything I could give her that would shed new light on his death.

She thanked me for seeing her and again said she felt I was the only one who understood how she felt. I told her how sorry I was that I had no new information for her. After she left, I felt I had failed her in some way. I felt even more so after I talked with her again a few days later. That is when she told me she had hired a private detective to look into the circumstances of her husband's death. She said it was costing her a fortune but she had to know the truth.

If I were writing this as fiction, I would tell you the detective found out how and why her husband had been murdered. But truth is, after several years and much money, he came up with zero. It was as she had been told. The young man had died of natural causes, and there was no foul play. I don't think she believed the detective, but she had spent more than too much money on this investigation.

I heard from her a few times after the PI's report, and she kept saying it just couldn't have happened as it did because they had so many plans for the future. But plans are just what they are—plans. We have no guarantees about the next day, the next hour, or even the next minute. It can all be over in a flash. I hope this young woman finally accepted that and moved on with her life.

Life is fickle. We can plan and plan but then come up against the wall of fate. Nothing in the future is for sure, which is why you have to live life in the moment.

## Sex, Dead Dogs, and Ed

Whenever I write or speak about how my book career got started, I never mention Ed Williams enough. Ed is a writer I met many years ago and well before I decided to write a book. He had burst on the scene with a collection of stories titled *Sex, Dead Dogs, and Me.* This was during the times when Lewis Grizzard was holding forth with stories gathered under hilarious titles. Ed saw that a catchy title was the key to success and added that in, along with the concept that sex sells, and named his opus accordingly.

I was reviewing books and movies for several papers in Georgia when I became aware of this book, which was written by a Macon author. I tracked Ed down and set up an appointment for an interview. When we met, it was friendship at first sight. Ed was one of the most gregarious, charming, and entertaining men I ever met. He had a story to tell and the promise of more to come. He was irreverent to the nth degree but made you smile and laugh even as you were shocked.

Later, I would attend events where Ed was signing books or making a speech, and I learned from him how to work a room. When the spotlight of Ed's personality fell on you, you felt you were the only person of importance there. He was focused, and with that focus came the charm. I have seen prim and proper little old ladies rush to his table to get him to autograph *Sex, Dead Dogs, and Me.* In my mind, I was thinking, do they know what they are getting? But they didn't care as they had come under the Ed Williams spell.

If I had to use one phrase to describe Ed, it would be "good old boy." He had his collection of buddies from high school and college, and they were do or die for each other. And if one of them was ready to party, well, then, they were all ready to party. I met some of Ed's buddies but I never joined the group. It was a closed band of brothers, and someone as conservative as I am would have just rained on their parade.

As Ed and I became better and better friends, he began to tell me I should write a book. He was the first person who planted the seed for that possibility. I thought he was crazy at first, but Ed wouldn't let the urging lag, and he prodded me with zeal. Later, my friends Jackie White and Milam Probst joined in the chorus of voices telling me "You have to write a book," and so I did.

When it came time to give my collection of stories a title, I thought about how important Ed's title had been to the success of his book. I let some pretty raunchy titles run through my mind before I cancelled those thoughts. Ed's sense of story content and mine were in two different places, and my Southern Baptist upbringing still influenced what I was willing to discuss and what I wasn't. So, I ended up titling my first book *Journey of a Gentle Southern Man.* I remember making my "title reveal" to Ed. He thought about it and told me it was perfect for stories from me. I guess Ed understood me as well as I did him.

Ed continued writing for a while, but now he has discovered a flair for photography. I have seen some of his pictures, and they are good, real good. He has a photographer's eye, and that is something you either have or you don't. I keep waiting for him to announce he has published a book of his photos. I am high on anticipation as to what the title will be.

## I Made a Vow

After I joined the Air Force and was processed through Officers Training School in San Antonio, Texas, I was assigned to Robins Air Force Base for my four-year military stint. I had been excited about seeing the world when I joined up, but my entire career was at that one base. The base was located adjacent to the town of Warner Robins, Georgia. It was fairly small, but I had access to Atlanta, which was only a hundred miles away.

When I move somewhere new, one of the first things I do is check out the local library. This meant I quickly asked if the base had a library and was pleasantly surprised to learn it did. I didn't wait long to search it out. It was a small building with a good supply of books. Most enjoyably, the library carried a lot of new fiction.

I didn't meet Mrs. Jarman, the head librarian, on my first or second visits. I did meet some of the staff who were manning the front desk. They were all nice people who seemed to love to read. I knew I had found some friends. As I talked with them, they mentioned Mrs. Jarman and how she was an expert on all things literary. This whetted my appetite to meet and have conversations with her.

On my third visit, she was there. She was a petite woman who looked and dressed the part of head librarian and also exuded Southern charm. I loved her from the moment I met her. All my life, I have been drawn to older women, and I have sought the friendship of many. I think this is because of the loss of my mother at an early age. As soon as I met Evelyn Jarman, I knew I wanted her as a friend.

And so began our friendship. I would get off work and head for the library. Generally, she would be in her office, and I would stick my head inside her door and say hello. Then it progressed to me seeking her out in her office and sitting down for conversations about books. Pretty soon, she began to tell me about the new fiction that was coming out and asking if I would like to reserve some of those books. I am a voracious reader, and I plowed through tons of books after I met her.

The fascinating thing about Mrs. Jarman was her talent as a conversationalist. We never ran out of things to talk about. Over the months that followed, I learned Mrs. Jarman had married during World War II. Her husband had joined the navy and was an officer who served overseas. When Mr. Jarman returned from the war, he had some difficulties adjusting to civilian life. I didn't know the term when she spoke of him to me, but he had what we now describe as PTSD (post-traumatic stress disorder).

Because of his problems, Mr. Jarman spent a lot of time hospitalized. She would talk about his visits home and also of his returns to the hospital. It was also around this time I began to notice some bruises on her wrists. I would ask her what she did to get bruised, and she would blame it on tripping or falling. She laughed about how clumsy she was, which I didn't buy at all, because she moved as gracefully as a swan.

One day when I went to visit her, she had a black eye. I was concerned when she again tried to brush it off. I pressed her, and she finally confided that her husband had had some bad moments, and in trying to calm him down, she ended up bruised. I was outraged she had suffered in any way, but she kept telling me he didn't mean to do it and stressed what a good man he was.

At a later time, she showed up with her arm in a sling and told me it was sprained. I was convinced it was broken but did not want to press her on it. I did tell her she should leave her husband for her own safety. Her response was that she would never leave him. When I asked why not, she responded by saying, "I made a vow."

She made a vow to love, honor, and cherish in sickness and in health, and it was a vow she was never going to break. If we were going to remain friends, I had to accept that as being the way things were and would be. And I did. I never asked her again to leave him. I just accepted that with him, there were good times and bad times.

Eventually, Mr. Jarman seemed to get better, or so his wife said. By this time, I had gotten married, and Terry, my wife, adored Mrs. Jarman. She insisted that I invite them both to dinner. Mrs. Jarman was hesitant at first and stated they did not go out. It was just the two of them and they stayed home. However, the next time I saw her, she said she had changed her mind and that if we still wanted them to come, they would.

It was a wonderful night. My wife sets a great table, and Mrs. Jarman oohed and aahed over everything in the nicest of ways. Mr. Jarman was a true Southern gentleman and was charming the entire evening. I liked him a lot. When it came time for the evening to end, I realized it had all passed too quickly. I hoped we could do it again. But we never did.

Shortly after that night, Mr. Jarman had an episode and had to go back into the hospital. It was a bad one, Mrs. Jarman told me. I don't think she had ever looked so fragile and vulnerable as she did that day. Still, she rallied and was soon back to recommending books for me to read.

Later, I accepted a job in California. I had always dreamed of going there. Mrs. Jarman approved. She said we should always follow our dreams. We talked a few times when I got started in California, but then she told me she was retiring. She said she thought Mr. Jarman would do better with her at home full time. I told her to be careful. "Always," she responded.

When we moved back from California, I tried to reach her through the library but was told she had asked not to have her home number given out. I didn't think I would ever hear from her again. It was in the early 1990s when I next heard from her. She called me at my office. She said she had heard my office was in the post office building in Macon and that she needed some stamps. She told me how many she needed and gave me an address to bring them to her.

I did as instructed and drove over to her house. After I knocked on the door, she answered it and came out on the porch. I gave her the stamps, and she gave me the exact amount of money they cost. I knew better than to decline the money. That was not her way. I asked about Mr. Jarman, and she said, "Not so good."

She said she had better get back inside, and I turned and started walking down her steps. I heard her say my name, so I turned and went back up the steps. She took my left wrist in her right hand and squeezed it. Then she said, "I want you to know you are very dear to me."

I said, "Me, too, Mrs. Jarman."

We never met again. Her number was unlisted, so I couldn't call, and when I decided to go back to the house, it was empty. She had simply faded away into the mists of time. I comforted myself with the memories I had of her. One situation stood out in my mind. It had happened a few months after we met. I had gone to lunch by myself, and, as I usually did, I took a book with me. As I made my way to a booth, I saw her sitting at a table. She was reading a book. She looked up, gave a little wave, and smiled. I went on to my booth and sat down. When she finished eating, she got up, looked my way, smiled, and left. I continued to read and eat.

The next time I saw her at the library, she told me she wanted to thank me. "For what?" I asked.

"For being a friend who respected my alone time," she said. "I have a need to have that kind of time."

Years after I delivered the stamps to her, a friend of mine who keeps up with obituaries called me one day and asked if I still knew the lady from the base library. I said I did, and he told me he had seen her obituary in the local newspaper earlier that week. I looked it up. Mrs. Jarman died on my birthday on September 13, 2007. I was sixty-six, she was ninety-two.

I learned a lot from Mrs. Jarman. I learned a lot about books and authors, I learned how to be a better friend, I learned how someone saying you are dear to them can make you feel like one of the most loved persons on earth, and I learned what true commitment in a marriage is. She had said she made a vow and that told me everything I needed to know.

## The Simplicity of Spring

If life is divided into four seasons, then the one we are born into is spring. Spring is the season of birth and the season of simplicity. I certainly can't remember being born, but I can remember how simple my life was when I was small. I lived in a cocoon of love. At least, I felt that way. I was the center of attention as the youngest of two children born to my parents.

I was born in 1941 and grew up in Clinton, South Carolina. Clinton was the poster child for the all-American town. It was a mill town (two cotton mills at least) and had no other major industries that I recall. It was a community composed of hard-working, fun-loving, church-going people.

My family was spread out all over the town. My uncle Lynn had a car dealership, my uncle Charlie ran a garage, my uncle Russell worked for my uncle Charlie at the garage, and my father was a bread salesman who drove a truck around town to the stores. My mother worked at Belk's as a salesperson until she and my father opened up a corner grocery store.

In my childhood memories, it is always spring or summer. I don't remember cold weather at all. Most of the time it is spring, and the dogwoods and the azaleas are blooming and the afternoons keep getting longer and longer. There was plenty of time for playing, and play we did. There were so many kids in the neighborhood. We played in front yards, backyards, and in the streets. We skated on the asphalt and skinned our knees over and over. Cars slowed down for us, and we moved over to let them pass.

Up the street from our house was where Judy Adair lived, my best friend from my neighborhood and still one of my best friends today. My best friend outside the neighborhood was Charles Tucker. I met him when he came to visit his grandmother, who lived across the street. We basically played with each other when he came to visit his grandmother and not with the other neighborhood kids. Tucker liked to play board games like Monopoly and Clue, and we could spend hours doing that without getting bored or tired at all.

Looming over all of it was my mother. She liked to talk and would hold me in her lap while sitting in a rocking chair and rock with me. As she did, she would tell one story after another. I heard stories about her life growing up in Gadsden, Alabama, and other stories about my daddy growing up in Clinton. I loved those stories and would beg for more. She also would sing to me songs such as "Danny Boy" and "Sonny Boy." She had a beautiful soprano voice and I could listen to it for hours.

My father was a playmate for me, too. Although he worked long, hard hours on the bread truck, when he finally got home I would meet him with the request of "Can we play?" Before he showered or even changed clothes, he would get down on the floor on his hands and knees and let me ride on his back around the living room and kitchen. He had a certain smell to him, a mixture of sweat and his own aroma. I loved that smell. It meant strength and security.

Those were the glory years, the simple years. I had no worries, had no fears. We weren't rich but we also weren't poor. In that two-bedroom, one-bathroom house on Holland Street, happiness lived and thrived. It was my spring, and though it was short, it is well remembered.

## The Significance of Summer

Four seasons of life—spring, summer, fall, and winter. If spring is a time of simplicity, then summer is a time of significance. In my own life, I had a very short spring. It ended when I was fourteen and my mother died. Then the summer season of my life began, and that meant I was mostly responsible for myself. I don't mean that I was suddenly required to provide for myself. I mean that after my mother died, I was responsible for the decisions of my life.

This was forced on me when I met with Mrs. Shouse, one of the teachers at my school. I was just entering tenth grade, and she suggested that instead of taking any electives that year that I fill the hours of my unrequired classes with eleventh-grade required classes. I needed twelve required classes to graduate. If I did this, I would finish the eleventh grade with eleven of my required classes and then I could take twelfth-grade English in summer school and start college in the fall of what would have been my senior year. She said to go home and discuss it with my father.

I knew that discussing it with my father would be him asking me what I wanted to do, and that would be it. Instead, I weighed the pros and cons. It would mean getting away from home, which was now a very sad place for me to be. It would also mean I would be starting college at sixteen and then quickly turning seventeen. It also meant I would not have any of the fun senior activities I had looked forward to doing.

In the end, I decided to stay in school for the full four years. I don't regret it. I think I made the wise decision. Of course, when it came time to go to college, I made my own choice. The only question my father had was how much it was going to cost. I don't blame him, we were on a limited income, so I couldn't opt for some high-priced college. I needed one that was moderate in cost and which would provide me with academic scholarships as well as a work scholarship. Erskine College filled the bill nicely.

The summer of my life had firmly set in, and I was responsible for selecting my major, choosing my courses, working my job(s), and getting some form of employment each summer. For spending money, my father sent me five dollars a week. I don't know how I did it, but I managed to have an active college life with that five dollars as my basic fund.

After law school, I went into the Air Force, and it was there I felt my summer really begin. I earned enough money to support myself. What a great feeling that was! I had made it. I had become an adult. I had money. I don't know if anybody else had that feeling of "I'm an adult" like I did. It was significant. Nobody could tell me what to do. I had the right to make all my own choices. Now, I am not saying I made all the right choices, but all the choices were mine.

And this was just the start. Just think of all the choices you make during the "summer" of your life. You pick a career. You pick a spouse. You pick a church. You pick when you want to have children. You learn the things that make you happy and the things that don't. From the sadness that initiated my "summer" until the time when I entered the "fall" of my life, I was happy. It had highs and lows, but overall, it was a happy, happy time for me.

I hope you can say the same. Someone asked me the other day if I had any regrets about my life. Was there anything I wish I had done that I didn't do. My answer was a quick no. My life, and especially my summer, was all I could have ever asked for, with a lot of extras I never expected. And that's the truth. My summer was significant in all the best ways.

## The Fruition of Fall

The summer of your life is the season to dream big and to plan and plan and plan. That's what I did. I remembered the words my mother used to whisper in my ear at night. She said, "You are special," and I believed her, oh, I believed her! And I believe that all of us are special in some sense of the word. There is no one I have ever met who I would say is just ordinary. No, inside us all is that special spark, and we just have to learn to give it free reign.

And after you do that and you reach the fall time of your life, it all pays off. I call it the fruition of fall, and I have been blessed with it over and over again. I have stated this before, and I will state it here again, I always wanted a secure family life and the ability to support that family. Once I had that, I had all the fruition I had prayed for every night. But God blessed me with more, much more.

I have loved movies since I was a small boy growing up in Clinton, South Carolina. For a small town, we were blessed with a couple of theaters. My mother loved the movies, and we went several times a week. It was cheap entertainment, and I loved the magic of what appeared on the screen. However, in my wildest dreams I never thought about being a movie critic. Still, somehow that evolved in my life, and when I reached the fall time, I was firmly ensconced in that field.

Writing a book was never on my radar either. I loved to read, and there were books in our house that my mother bought, and there was the great Presbyterian College library where non-collegiate people could also go. I grew up on the writings of Thomas B. Costain, James Michener, Lloyd C. Douglas, Betty Smith, Margaret Mitchell, and many others. In the summertime, during the hottest times of the day, I would lie on my parents' bed, the windows open, reading with the fan blowing on me. It was paradise.

Many years later, my friends Ed Williams, Jackie White, and Milam Propst encouraged me to put my "stories" into a book. I had been doubtful, but their support gave me the right push. And after I had my first book, *Journey of a Gentle Southern Man*, published, God sent me a sign I was on the right track.

It came after a book signing I had had in a town outside Atlanta. It had been fairly successful, and I was feeling good about it, but I was also ready to get back home to Perry. I was already in my car when a man approached me and knocked on the window. It was summer and I had already turned on the air conditioning and had my windows rolled up. I rolled down the one on the driver's side, and the man leaned in towards me and told me that he had been told by God to tell me He had a lot of good things in store for me. I didn't know how to reply, and I don't think I said anything except for maybe a thanks.

And with that the man turned and walked away.

It took me a moment to come to my senses, and then I started going back over the last hour or so. I realized the man had been in the area where I was, and he was helping set up and advising people as to where things were located. I had introduced myself to him, but we had not had a long conversation. Still, since I had seen him, his approaching my car did not alarm me.

On the drive home, I mulled over these events and decided I would take this message to heart. I decided to keep taking chances and try for higher and higher goals as I continued my writing career. And it has led me to eight books. God certainly did have a lot in store for me.

Enjoy the spring and summer sessions of your life and know that in the fall of your years, those efforts and dreams of your earlier days will come to fruition. Some may be large payoffs while others may be smaller. And some may even be setbacks. But if you are as blessed and lucky as I have been, you will see your talents grow and your opportunities develop.

The fruition of fall is a time of reaping the crops sown in your earlier years.

# Chapter 6

# The Wisdom of Winter

Winter has arrived. At least the winter of my life has entered my door. As I write this, I am eighty years old, the age of winter in anyone's book. How did it get here so fast? I know, I know, that is what everyone says who reaches the age of eighty. But it did seem to get here in the blink of an eye.

So clearly I remember being sixteen and sitting on the pavement of Stonewall Street in front of my friend Agnes's house. For some reason, we were talking about age, and I asked her if she ever thought about getting old. I remember particularly asking her what she thought it felt like to be forty. At that time, forty seemed to be an ancient age. Agnes took out a pack of cigarettes, gave me one, lit up, and blew out a smoke ring. She then said she was going to be young forever. I agreed that was a good plan.

But eventually forty did arrive, and it hit me hard. I don't know why that age was so significant. Maybe because that was my mother's age when she died. I remember when it occurred to me that I had lived longer than she did. But then came fifty, sixty, and seventy, and they were not that big a thing. Eighty was a definite year of transition. I realized I was in the winter of my life and that everything was tentative.

Still, I wake up each morning wondering what the day will bring. I do this in a positive sense and not a negative one.

Whatever is coming out of the blue, I think it will be good. That goes back to that mantra I have quoted over and over. "Anticipation is a joyful thing but expectation will kill you."

As I look back over the journey of my life, I realize that winter does bring wisdom. I have learned life lessons. I have also come to realize that my belief is that God has a framework for our lives. He has a plan. But it is up to us to make the decisions inside the framework. My framework was to get an education, get married, have kids, keep my faith steady, have a solid job. All the extras were when I colored in between the lines.

I have always dared to dream. Once I got my first movie review published in a paper, I was off to the races. If one paper liked me, then why wouldn't twenty others? And if I was in the newspapers, then I should also be able to be on radio. And if I was on radio, then why wouldn't I be on television? And if I was on television, then why couldn't I be on the internet?

A woman told me the other day her thirteen-year-old son loved movies and wanted to be me. She then asked how could he become me. I explained how in today's world, there were so many opportunities for the Jackie K. Coopers of the world. You can set up your own YouTube channel, Instagram account, TikTok account, and more. It amazes me that kids today can dream all kinds of dreams and are not tied down with certain stereotypes of success.

Another thing I have learned over the course of my journey is the importance of friends. It is amazing to have friends for twenty, thirty, forty, fifty years. These are the ones who know who you are and have remained steady in your life.

That is why I love the internet. It provides a way to keep in touch with people who live far away from me.

So, when you live to the age that you enter the winter of your life, hold on to the thought that you have amassed some wisdom along the way. It may be huge treasures of information that you can draw upon in the present or maybe small nuggets of intelligence you have used in the past. If you get the chance, share what you have learned, as it might make someone's life easier.

## Afterword

And now it is done. This book is finished. I started it when I was on the edge of eighty, and now I have fully dunked myself into that ocean. Come on in, the water's fine. It is just a part of life like every other age has been.

As I reflect back on the journey of this book, I realize I am still a hale and hearty member of "The Four-F Club." Faith, family, friends, and food still enrich my life in a million different ways. I have also discovered that I have new friends of my old age. It is so true that one never becomes too old to add a new friend. I could rattle off a list of people I am close to now that I didn't even know existed when I started this book.

Are there more stories to tell in this journey of my life? I think so. Every day is a new adventure and every second is precious. I wake with anticipation as to what wonders will unfold for me in this new time period. I am full of anticipation, not expectation, because I take nothing for granted. Life is what it is, when it is, how it is.

But until we meet again, in one form or fashion, I leave you with these words—love God, love your family, love and cherish your friends, and have yourself a good meal.

Blessings on you all.

## The Author

JACKIE K. COOPER is the author of seven books. As a movie and book critic his reviews can be found online on his YouTube channel and social media pages. Cooper is a member of the Broadcast Film Critics Association and one of the founders of the Southeastern Film Critics Association.